ROMANTIC
Style

Better Homes and Gardens® Books ◆ Des Moines, Iowa

BETTER HOMES AND GARDENS® BOOKS ◆ AN IMPRINT OF MEREDITH® BOOKS

Romantic Style

EDITOR: *Linda Hallam*

SENIOR ASSOCIATE DESIGN DIRECTOR: *Richard Michels*

CONTRIBUTING EDITORS: *Andrea Caughey, Diane Carroll, Susan Dowell, Carla Howard, Linda Krinn, Tangi Schaapveld, Colleen Scully*

COPY CHIEF: *Terri Fredrickson*

COPY AND PRODUCTION EDITOR: *Victoria Forlini*

EDITORIAL OPERATIONS MANAGER: *Karen Schirm*

MANAGERS, BOOK PRODUCTION: *Pam Kvitne, Marjorie J. Schenkelberg*

CONTRIBUTING COPY EDITOR: *Jane Woychick*

CONTRIBUTING PROOFREADERS: *Susan Burgess, Beth Lastine, Jennifer Mitchell, Shelley H. Stewart*

CONTRIBUTING PHOTOGRAPHERS: *Gordon Beall, Bill Holt*

ILLUSTRATOR: *Cathie Bleck*   INDEXER: *Kathleen Poole*

ELECTRONIC PRODUCTION COORDINATOR: *Paula Forest*

EDITORIAL AND DESIGN ASSISTANTS: *Kaye Chabot, Mary Lee Gavin*

MEREDITH® BOOKS

EDITOR IN CHIEF: *James D. Blume*

DESIGN DIRECTOR: *Matt Strelecki*

MANAGING EDITOR: *Gregory H. Kayko*

EXECUTIVE EDITOR, HOME DECORATING AND DESIGN: *Denise L. Caringer*

DIRECTOR, SALES, SPECIAL MARKETS: *Rita McMullen*

DIRECTOR, SALES, PREMIUMS: *Michael A. Peterson*

DIRECTOR, SALES, RETAIL: *Tom Wierzbicki*

DIRECTOR, BOOK MARKETING: *Brad Elmitt*

DIRECTOR, OPERATIONS: *George A. Susral*

DIRECTOR, PRODUCTION: *Douglas M. Johnston*

VICE PRESIDENT AND GENERAL MANAGER: *Douglas J. Guendel*

BETTER HOMES AND GARDENS® MAGAZINE

EDITOR IN CHIEF: *Karol DeWulf Nickell*

EXECUTIVE BUILDING EDITOR: *Joan McCloskey*

EXECUTIVE INTERIOR DESIGN EDITOR: *Sandra S. Soria*

MEREDITH PUBLISHING GROUP

PRESIDENT, PUBLISHING GROUP: *Stephen M. Lacy*

VICE PRESIDENT-PUBLISHING DIRECTOR: *Bob Mate*

MEREDITH CORPORATION

CHAIRMAN AND CHIEF EXECUTIVE OFFICER: *William T. Kerr*

CHAIRMAN OF THE EXECUTIVE COMMITTEE: *E.T. Meredith III*

All of us at Better Homes and Gardens® Books are dedicated to providing you with information and ideas to enhance your home. We welcome your comments and suggestions. Write to us at: Better Homes and Gardens Books, Home Decorating and Design Editorial Department, 1716 Locust St., Des Moines, IA 50309-3023.

If you would like to purchase any of our home decorating and design, cooking, crafts, gardening, or home improvement books, check wherever quality books are sold. Or visit us at: bhgbooks.com
Cover Photograph: Gordon Beall

A LITTLE ROMANCE

On a warm June afternoon, I fell in love—with Paris, one of the world's most romantic and beautiful cities. From the tall casement windows of our tiny Left Bank hotel, I watched the wonderful old city wake each morning. From the bridges that cross the Seine, I watched the sun set each day. In between, I toured the art museums and sculpture-filled gardens and wandered through the shops that line grand boulevards and cobblestone streets.

On the flight home, reading French decorating magazines, I resolved to create a book of pretty rooms and gentle settings, a romantic escape that also would be filled with decorating ideas. Little did I know then how easy and enjoyable it would be to find the lovely, very personal homes that you will visit on these pages. In fact, the only dilemma in this pleasant task was choosing from among the wealth of charming locations brimming with ideas and inspiration. As we worked, the plethora of romantic-style homes began to make sense to us.

In this age of high-tech hurry, romantic style is a soothing balm for decorating enthusiasts across the country—in cities, small towns, and rural settings. The owners we met along the way have very different interpretations, yet all share the philosophy of designing a unique home that's a refuge from the busy world. From each location, we gleaned decorating inspiration, advice, sources—and new friends. To each of our generous homeowners, a grateful thank-you—or perhaps more appropriately, merci beaucoup.

LINDA HALLAM, EDITOR, ROMANTIC STYLE

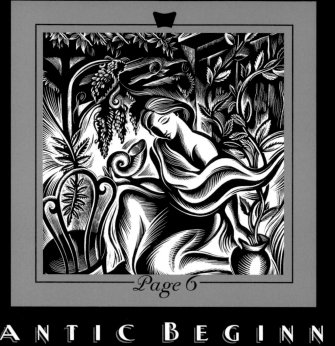

Page 6

ROMANTIC BEGINNINGS

INSPIRED BY ROMANCE

Page 14

GRACIOUS LIVING

Page 150

ELEGANT DINING

Page 172

ROMANTIC BEDROOMS

Page 192

Sources, page 212 ◆ *Index, page 214*

ROMANTIC BEGINNINGS

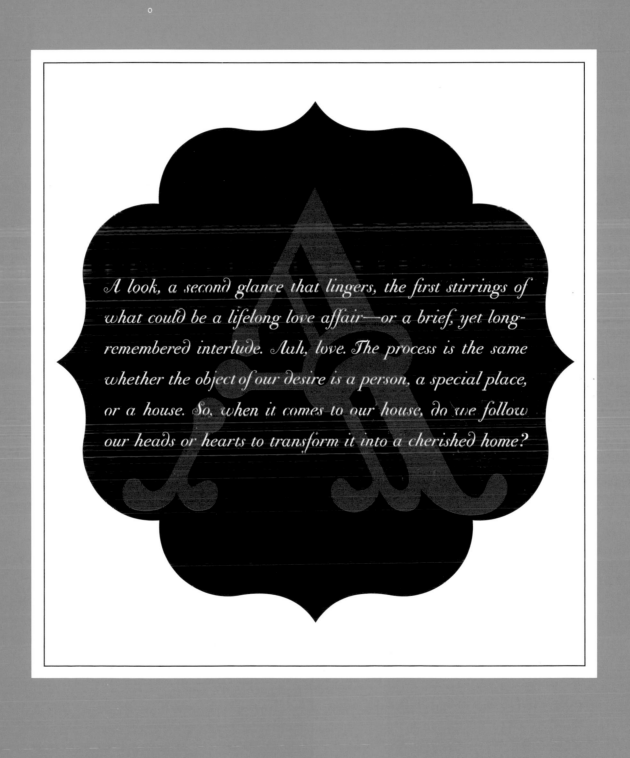

A look, a second glance that lingers, the first stirrings of what could be a lifelong love affair—or a brief, yet long-remembered interlude. Auh, love. The process is the same whether the object of our desire is a person, a special place, or a house. So, when it comes to our house, do we follow our heads or hearts to transform it into a cherished home?

Romance is the zest of life, an experience eternally young and always new.
It's the thrill of imagination—what other word conjures up such pleasant images
of sunshine, flowers, candlelight, music, and soft whispers? And what other word
expresses the most enduring feelings and longings?

Romance—and romantic-style decorating—always wait, ready to soften and to
soothe. In times of rapid change, romantic movements in fashion, art, literature,
music, and design offer a respite, a comforting pause in a world that moves too fast.
The late-19th and early-20th centuries, eras of industrialization and urbanization,
saw successive romantic movements, from ornate Victorian styles to the sensuous
nature motifs of Art Nouveau and Arts and Crafts. Earlier, English poets and
painters recalled an idealized past in response to the harshness of early industrial life.
Before the French Revolution, French aristocrats, burdened by the intrigues and
elaborate rituals of court life, relaxed in charming pastoral settings.

Although the homes and interiors of the past
undoubtedly are interesting in decorative arts history,
romantic styles always liberally interpret, never

ROMANCE IS *Eternally* YOUNG AND FOREVER NEW

ROMANCE ALWAYS WAITS TO *Soften* AND TO SOOTHE

strictly re-create the past. Scandinavian furnituremakers and artisans simplified French influences to create the soft curves and pale furniture that are beautiful interpretations of the romantic. The light painted finishes and mirrored sconces that reflect candlelight brighten the long nights of Scandinavian winters. In the more temperate climates of the British Isles, romantic styles are associated with cottages as well as castles, and with gardens and floral motifs. Warmed by strong sunlight, earthy, mellow colors are hallmarks of Italian, Spanish, and Portuguese romanticism.

In a world increasingly without borders, romantic-style decorators freely mix many countries and periods, and antique, vintage, and reproduction pieces to achieve a more personal look. Decorators may gravitate to all-white or creamy rooms, serene and peaceful in the absence of color or patterns. Or they may pair florals and patterns for playful cottage interpretations. Asian and African pieces, too, find homes in the rich cultural mix that exemplifies romantic style.

Because style is so individual, small touches can be enough to give existing rooms a more romantic mood. Decorating enthusiasts often start with their bedrooms, their most private spaces. Accents as simple as new linens, sheers or lace curtains, and a skirted bedside table quickly create a romantic mood. If walls are dark, repainting them in a pale, pretty color, such as seashell pink, apple green, or creamy white, totally changes the ambience. Furniture, too, takes on an entirely different spirit when it's painted white or lightly distressed.

In living and dining rooms, it's easy to invite romance by slipcovering dark upholstered pieces in white cotton or replacing heavy, tailored window treatments with sheers or lace panels. As in the bedroom, painting walls and woodwork in pale tones often is all that's necessary to transform the look. Other easy changes include adding accent pillows made from vintage fabrics and trims, grouping black and white family photographs in decorative silver frames on a table, hanging botanicals or other floral prints or decoratively framed mirrors, and replacing overhead light fixtures with evocative chandeliers. A vase of fresh flowers is the ideal finishing touch.

Outside, romantic touches may include a garden sculpture or decorative birdbath. Or romance can be as simple and effective as hanging a candle chandelier from a tree or porch beam or lighting rustic garden torches or lanterns made for chunky candles. Floral cloths over a patio table, cushions, and pillows can complete the appealing scene. This pretty style is waiting for you to create. And enjoy.

ROMANCE
LIBERALLY
INTERPRETS THE
Charms OF
GENTLE AGES

INSPIRED BY ROMANCE

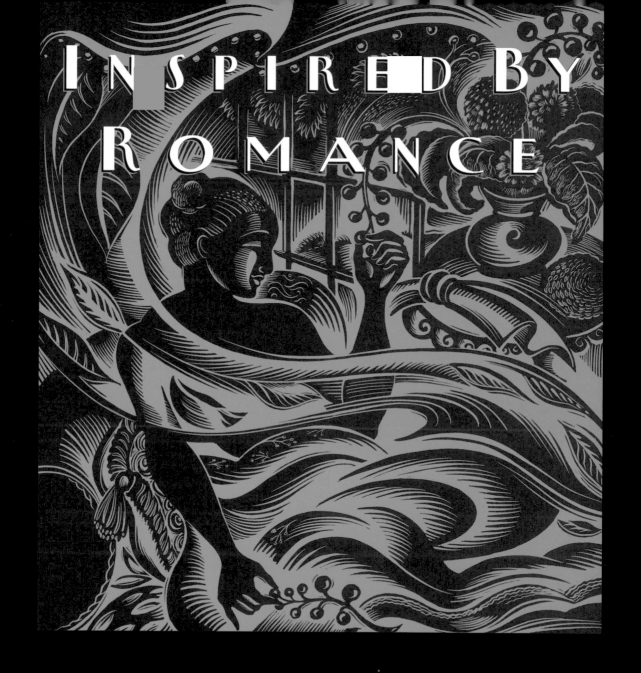

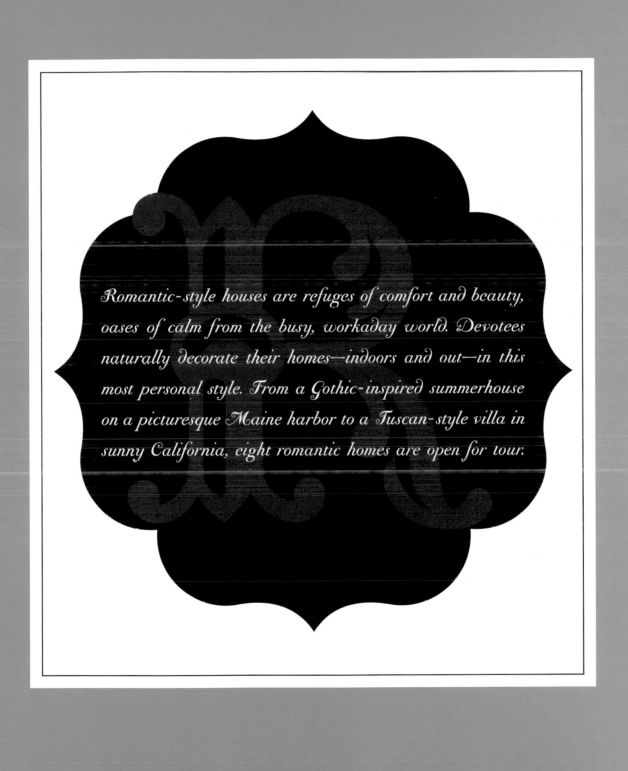

Romantic-style houses are refuges of comfort and beauty, oases of calm from the busy, workaday world. Devotees naturally decorate their homes—indoors and out—in this most personal style. From a Gothic-inspired summerhouse on a picturesque Maine harbor to a Tuscan-style villa in sunny California, eight romantic homes are open for tour:

SONOMA
COTTAGE
REBORN

A California couple resurrects a 100-year-old Sonoma cottage for their home. In this pastoral valley, they live in sunlit rooms decorated with delicately painted French and Italian country furniture and vintage finds. Mirrors reflect lovely rooms illuminated at dusk by crystal chandeliers as beautiful as fine art. Cherubs impart their own notes of grace and sweet tidings to the peaceful scene.

Through the sunny, mild Sonoma Valley days, rooms glow in luminous sunlight. As twilight approaches, the warm light is gloriously tinted in shades of pink and pale amber. By twilight, chandeliers sparkle as the golden candlelight and softly alluring shadows romance the rooms.

Lorraine and Ben Egidio journeyed from the East Coast to the West Coast and through a number of houses and design styles to arrive at this lovely setting. "We wanted to create a sense of simplicity and beauty at the same time," Lorraine says. "I found it when we eliminated colors and started living with white."

By the time the couple purchased the 100-year-old house and adjoining property for a bed-and-breakfast, they wanted to swap their English antiques and dark wood for a lighter look—one that would incorporate the Italian furnishings they prefer. Ben designed a charming addition to open the house to light and views, and Lorraine had the wood-clad walls and ceilings drywalled and painted white. They added Italian light fixtures, including a painted wooden chandelier in the breakfast room and an ornate iron-and-crystal chandelier in the dining room.

Lorraine chose primarily French and Italian furniture, including some vintage reproductions noteworthy for their sculptural lines. She purchased other painted pieces and painted reproductions. The French bed with applied trim, once a dark, sober piece, was transformed into the creamy white anchor of the serene master bedroom.

Paint also works its magic in the delightful breakfast room. Here, Lorraine restyled, painted, and distressed an American stepback cabinet for needed storage. And she pulled off her decorating pièce de résistance with thrift-shop 1940s reproduction Louis XVI-style chairs, transforming them with white paint and upholstery fabric. The all-white rooms are beautiful, but not fragile or precious. Because Ben and Lorraine enjoy entertaining family and friends, accessories are minimal and restricted to a collection of cherubs and statues that show the patina of age. Mirrors, chosen for their sizes and decorative frames, reflect light and calm views from room to room. "We found the house and gravitated to white at the same time," Lorraine says. "I didn't want to live with a lot of color anymore, but I do want to live with light and what I love. We do that here every day."

In the living room,
a candleholder from an
estate sale and
a candelabra illuminate
the tapestry. The
custom-designed
sideboard reflects French
and Italian influences.

Gentle SETTINGS WELCOME PLAYFUL OBJECTS OF

OPPOSITE: *An informal pairing of objects brings balance to the mantel in the all-white living room graced by an English secretary.* **ABOVE LEFT:** *Crystals swing from the gilded metal chandelier in the dining room.* **ABOVE RIGHT:** *The mirror frame and lamp detailing contrast with the rugged Greco-Roman-style horse.*

Mirrors, framed in gilded metal or creamy white, reflect light and views from room to room. A rug in the French Aubusson style complements the French table and Italian chairs.

TAUPE *Gently* AGE WHITE ROOMS.

ROMANTIC Style is...

Beauty is forever—in objects that have escaped the ravages of time as well as in those that proudly show their years. Romantic style values beauty wherever it is found, from garden flowers and simple glazed terra-cotta to sculptures lovely in their classical motifs and poses.

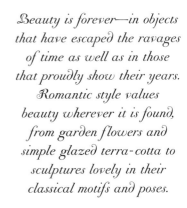

CLASSICAL FIGURES, FOREVER *Graceful* IN REPOSE

Gentle settings welcome playful objects of love and sensuous shapes of curves and scrolls. The shy innocence of cherubs and the ardor of lovebirds symbolize the joy of young love. Classical motifs recall the enduring qualities of beauty and art unaffected by the passage of time.

GENTLE BIRDS CROONING *Sweet* SONGS

SHIMMERING ETCHED AND *Crystal* GLASSES

DELICATE WHITE FLOWERS AND *Topiaries* IMPART *Garden* TOUCHES TO PRISTINE SETTINGS.

A white pedestal vase filled with tulips contributes a relaxed accent in the breakfast room. OPPOSITE: *White paint and fabric update reproduction Louis XVI chairs.*

LEFT: *Lorraine Egidio painted the vintage bed as the anchor for her bedroom. A needlepoint rug adds delicate color.* **ABOVE RIGHT:** *An Italian chair, discreetly aged with paint, pairs with the French vanity.* **BELOW RIGHT:** *The white porcelain classical figure echoes the column motif of the cast table base.*

CANDLES AND CANDLESTICKS

Shimmering candlelight creates the ambience of romantic style. No matter how beautiful the chandelier or exquisite the lamp, candlelight illuminates rooms with a glow and mystery unattainable from any other light source. Candlesticks and candelabra, beautiful in their materials and shapes, evoke memories of romantic dinners, quiet conversations, dancing for two, and sweet goodnights. For a collector, a shapely candelabra incorporating cherubs or angels inspires love at first sight. As with romance, follow your heart and collect what you love.

LOUISIANA
LAKE
VIEWS

Surrounded by old pecan orchards and cotton fields, on family land known as Locustland Plantation, an artist and her family built their home. She turns to nature and her garden as inspiration for art and for the polished interiors that frame views of long summer days and gently changing seasons. The result is a welcoming home evocative of the state's refined art and legendary hospitality.

RED WALLS DRAMATIZE *Art* AND SET A *Festive* MOOD FOR DINING.

At the end of the long drive, in the garden on the lake, the city is far away. The days are long, hot, often humid; the nights warm, balmy, and still. Stars light the clear, dark sky and in the morning, birds and insects sing to the waking world.

The contrast between the wildness of the natural environment and the refinement of classical art is a strong one in Louisiana, a state associated with the exquisitely detailed bird paintings of John James Audubon and with evocatively romantic landscape paintings. "Nature fascinates me; a leaf or stone can be as beautiful as a painting," Becky Vizard says. "Our home isn't decorated in a style or a period or a theme. It's a weekend house that my husband, Michael, and our children Sarah and Ross live in every day with the art and furnishings that mean something to us. I have to have a rapport with something to buy it, whether it is furniture or a painting. I never buy to fill up space. We wait until something is right."

Living and experiencing are the essential concepts behind Becky's version of romantic decorating. Furnished with French and Italian antiques collected one by one through the years, and with inherited family pieces of varying pedigrees, not one of the rooms is off-limits to children or dogs. Richly ornamented fabrics, which Becky buys in France for her antique textile business, cover a console in the vermilion-red living and dining room. As pillow covers, the fabrics accent the sofa where Michael's hunting dog often lounges.

Because of the home's private location, downstairs windows are bare. Hanging with paintings by artist friends is an 18th-century drawing of Ceres, the Roman goddess of agriculture, whose images Becky collects. But the ever-changing views of the garden and lake, framed by French doors, are the most striking art. On an interior wall of the breakfast room, the family's orientation to nature is evident in the framed entomology boards, once used in a classroom, displayed alongside a Louis Philippe mirror from France. Seashells substitute for decorative hangers.

Upstairs, the bleached oak floors and pale walls are soft backdrops for the inherited Louisiana-made plantation bed and Italian furniture. Furnishings are edited to create rooms where nature and art are paramount. "In Louisiana, our lives are so influenced by the outdoors, it's only natural that our house would be," Becky says.

Inherited dining chairs, updated with flirty skirted slipcovers, pair with a country-style table in the open living and dining room. Dutch botanical prints echo the nature theme.

LEFT: *A pair of armless French love seats flanks an antique pine cupboard with a fruitwood finish. Pillows are made of antique fabrics and trims.*
ABOVE RIGHT: *A drawing of the angel Gabriel hangs above the console.*
BELOW RIGHT: *Abstract art by Beth Lambert of New Orleans introduces a contemporary element.*

The seashell-encrusted
picture frame and patterned pillows introduce exotic touches
in the relaxed sitting room. The antique bench,
a wedding gift from Michael Vizard's sister, serves as a
sturdy coffee table. Flowers hint at the garden outside.

*rt transforms the
upstairs sitting room into a gallery, highlighted by the
Italian silk pendent light. White cotton slipcovers,
with pillows from Becky Vizard's textile collection, and
sheer draperies bespeak a mood of endless summer.*

Romantic Style is...

The most passionate romances often are the most unexpected—when opposites attract with tempestuous but thrilling results. So too in decorating when refined materials, of beautiful fabrics and intricate trim, tame rooms of rustic walls and rugged floors.

EUROPEAN *Brocades,* FINE SILKS, GARDEN HATS

Small, graceful touches imbue everyday life with a sense of celebration. From fresh garden or grocery store flowers to a reminder of a favorite pet to handsome bottles for spirits, extra embellishments add the ease and small graces that soften the rough edges of life.

Golden EMBROIDERY, WHITE FLOWERS

SHELL PINK *Frosted* GLASS BOTTLES, IRON SCROLLS

An iron chandelier, found in a New Orleans shop, illuminates a fruitwood table from France and gently aged Italian-made chairs. Peonies impart a feel of the early spring garden.

GRACIOUSLY *Anchors* A LAKESIDE DINING ROOM.

With a decorative shell to cover its hook, a finely detailed entomology board hangs with a Louis Philippe mirror above the French fruitwood buffet. An urn displays a topiary.

The charms of French Louisiana include tile floors, earthy colors, and rustic pottery, all in evidence in this country house north of New Orleans.
ABOVE LEFT: A French wire basket holds towels above the old-fashioned claw-foot tub in the master bath. **ABOVE:** Dried garden flowers and Turkish olive oil jars enliven the breezeway that doubles as a potting shed.
BELOW LEFT: Thoughtful arrangement converts walking sticks, vintage watering cans, and topiaries into an artful display.

Sweet peas spill from a glass urn. OPPOSITE: *A mix of furniture, from a Louisiana-made bed with the traditional tester top to French and Italian pieces, resides in the master bedroom.*

IN A ROOM WITH A *View*, A

A CARVED ANGEL WATCHES OVER A *Grand* PLANTATION BED.

Love Notes

FOR THE LOVE OF NATURE

The beauty of the outdoors is the art of the world. If one could walk into a painting, perhaps the experience would be comparable to a nature lover's fascination with forests, rivers, and gardens. The colors and patterns of the environment inspire and delight as they challenge the skills of artists and illustrators. Seashells, created by their inhabitants and polished by sand and sea, and butterflies with wings of brief beauty, surpass human imagination and artistic skill.

Invite nature inside and savor the beauty of simplicity.

Artwork and Artifacts

Working with her family, a Washington, D.C. artist finds beauty in the old and neglected, in houses and objects that show the patina and character of age. She restores houses as theatrical backgrounds for sentimental furnishings, favorite art, and her ever-changing collections. A farmhouse-style cottage on a quiet city street creates an evocative setting for family living.

SOFT *Colors* REMINISCENT OF AGED PARCHMENT ALLOW *Treasures* TO STAR.

For their current city restoration, Maureen O'Brien and Jeff Sandmann work with monochromatic backgrounds in shades of white, cream, and naturals that allow their edited furniture, accessories, collections, and art to change at will. Constant is Maureen's ironstone collection, neglected pieces chosen for their patinas and paired with bits of calligraphy.

The avocation for restoration fits neatly with Maureen's decorating philosophy, which assigns a theme, often inspired by travel, to each of her rooms. Their narrow farmhouse-style cottage built in 1922 required such flights of fantasy to overcome the lack of architectural detailing. The living room at the front of the house features a mix of low tables and a Tibetan manuscript as the major art, evoking for Maureen the faded elegance of war-torn France in the 1940s. "The dark colors and lack of natural light remind me of photographs I've seen of Paris," she says.

Equally imaginative is the constantly changing dining room. A bit of red wrapping paper, printed in Germany, and roses may set a tone for three months; a green Chianti wine bottle, shaped like a fish, could spark a month-long foray into shades of green and frosted glass. Sometimes a small object Maureen finds or the subject she paints that day takes the dining room in a new, albeit temporary, direction.

The hand-painted floor makes a more permanent statement in the sunny sitting room with windows on three sides. To age the room, Maureen painted the floor with a faux-graining technique to emulate wood; she added further detail with 2,000 hand-painted nail motifs. Furnishings include a large mirror found in a Victorian home the couple previously restored, a chandelier made into a floor lamp by a woodworker friend, and a contemporary chaise with Zen-like simplicity.

Upstairs, romance veers east and west with daughter Lauren's French-style bedroom, inspired by a trip to Paris, and Maureen and Jeff's coolly serene Asian-style bedroom, recalling the year Jeff traveled in the Far East. Outside, Maureen designed and painted a Tuscan-themed loggia for casual dining and entertaining.

Melding the mix of cultures and styles together are sentimental family objects, with artifacts sprinkled throughout. "We have things from our relatives, such as an incense burner, that make it into every house we live in," adds Maureen. "We like the spirits of many lives in our houses."

A 19th-century mirror, found in the family's previous home, imparts dramatic scale in the sitting room. Touches of playful leopard-print fabric update the antique furniture.

LEFT: *Pale fabrics unify an eclectic mix of French, Victorian, and Asian-inspired furniture in the sunny sitting room.*
ABOVE RIGHT: *A French dressmaker's armature pairs with a prim American Gothic Revival chair in its original red velvet.*
BELOW RIGHT: *A battered cabinet displays a garden planter.*

EACH ROOM *Filled* WITH ELEMENTS OF AGE SPINS A

TALE OF ROMANCE AND *Mystery.*

Visions of Tuscany inspired the curtained loggia with columns decoratively painted to emulate aged stucco. Woven chairs with leather seats and trim are from Mexico.

ROMANTIC *Style* is...

Gentle sunlight warms rooms of treasures new and old. Alabaster, glass, crystal, and silver meld harmoniously into settings enriched by vintage finds and sentimental family treasures. Fragile crystals suspend like raindrops from delicate leaves. A bird's nest is nature's work of art.

CUT CRYSTAL, OLD SILVER, ALABASTER, *Gold,* AND BRONZE

In rooms of white flowers, dragonflies flit on sparkling wings, tiny drawers conceal treasures of a bygone time, and handwriting preserves an era when pen and ink created beauty in delicate lettering and elaborate flourishes. Objects of long ago share their faded charms.

Flutes OF CHAMPAGNE TO CELEBRATE SPECIAL DAYS

TOUCHES OF THE *hand*, RED WINE, DRAGONFLIES

THE DINING ROOM WARM WHITER *Shades* OF PALE.

LEFT: *Slipcovered wing chairs and an oak server anchor a dining room presided over by a tulle-dressed mannequin. Tulle repeats as a soft accent for the electrified chandelier. Abstract gift wrap from Germany hangs as art from a curtain tieback.* **RIGHT:** *Beaded napkin rings dress up the festive place settings and linens.*

ouches of Asia, inspired
by Jeff Sandmann's travels in the Far East, create serenity
in the sparely furnished master bedroom. Soft
color and minimum accessories soothe with calm and order.
Bamboo and orchids introduce natural elements.

A trip to Paris gave Maureen's daughter Lauren the impetus for a youthful bedroom with definite French accents. The acid green, hot pink, and purple scheme refreshes vintage furnishings with touches of satin and florals.

Language Of Romance

Love Notes

Words record the stories of romance—poetry, myth, legend, fact, and the most famous fiction. Words translate aspiration into expression, spelling out in their letters the thoughts and passions of their writers and perhaps their readers. Love letters or little notes, which the French poetically call billet doux, are saved and cherished through the years. So, too, are the fond notes of friends or the first childish scrawls a mother lovingly preserves. The touch of the hand and the curves of calligraphy make words all the more beautiful, turning writing into art.

FAIRIES
AND
FLOWERS

Playful fairies join the family as welcome visitors for a summer at Rosecliffe Cottage, an enchanting Carpenter Gothic-style house and English garden on the coast of Maine. The charm of picturesque 19th-century American summerhouses in New England inspired the talented owner to design a fantasy retreat filled with antique furnishings, 19th-century Impressionist art, and collected treasures that delight her children, grandchildren, and friends.

FISH WITH FLOWERS *Dance* ON A *Country* SIDEBOARD SET FOR LUNCH.

Along the rocky coast, rugosa roses growing on seaside cliffs give an old house its lovely new name. Its owner's favorite childhood books, including *A Day in Fairyland*, and her inherited and assembled collections set the evocative and personal decorating direction. Alabaster lamps and delicate Victorian painted papier-mâché furniture against backgrounds of vintage pine walls and ceilings contribute romantic touches that recall English country gardens, American seaside retreats, and woodsy Adirondack lodges.

For the dining room, Cornelia Smithwick chose a vintage lilac-and-hydrangea-print fabric to complement her mother's collections of antique majolica and pink transferware. Cornelia found the Welsh cupboard in the English Cotswolds; she mixed in a cherry table and casual twig dining chairs from New England to evoke the garden. In keeping with the floral theme, the interior designer framed a rare 19th-century stump needlework panel to hang over the sideboard.

Florals are equally evident in the living room, where tea-stained, rose-print slipcovers set a summery mood in contrast to the dark paneling. The Victorian glass and metal fixture, too, is dressed for summer with muslin, as was traditional in the 19th and early 20th centuries. Antique vases brim with garden flowers through the summer months.

The sunny yellow kitchen, remodeled with Gothic-style detailing, and the adjoining breakfast room are light, bright spaces, oriented to the views of the harbor. Flowered fabric enhances the charm.

Bedrooms tell their own stories. The attic with its Gothic casement windows is the playfully designated "Faerie Aerie," designed for Cornelia's granddaughters. This floor houses her repository of fairy books and frolicking figurines.

One floor below, the Stagwold bedroom is aptly named after a stag spotted during remodeling. A lime-oak bed with a Gothic-style headboard and brackets from London anchor a room that houses stag memorabilia collected through the years. The camel and cream colors work with the tailored theme of the room. Despite the many comforts of the interior, Cornelia and her guests spend as much time as possible on the porch with views of the sea and harbor. "I adore the house and garden, but the ever-changing harbor with sailboats and the misty coast are the true romance of the house," she says.

Rare American stump work needlecraft hangs above a country-style sideboard in the dining room. Garden flowers spill from antique carp vases; a twig basket holds bread.

A decoupaged
Victorian screen serves
as art in the dining
room. Tie-on cushions
update the twig chairs,
which are painted in
two colors for a more
casual feeling.

A rugged Welsh cupboard brims with a collection of inherited 19th-century majolica from England. Summer garden flowers casually fill the white pitcher, an antiquing find.

RUSTIC TWIG CHAIRS AND *Botanical* MOTIFS SET A *Mood* OF ADIRONDACK SUMMER CAMPS.

ABOVE LEFT: *A burnt-bamboo table displays a Victorian shell box.* **BELOW LEFT:** *The Gothic-style breakfront organizes collected black and white Staffordshire spaniels.* **RIGHT:** *An American Impressionist painting hangs over the mantel. Muslin covers the Victorian light fixture in old-fashioned summer-house style.*

Romantic Style is...

The charms of the Scottish highlands, the English Cotswolds, and New England summer retreats epitomize Victorian escape from city life. Endearing figurines, from shepherds to hunters dressed in tartan kilts, are happy reminders of long high summer in the civilized wilds.

STAFFORDSHIRE SHEPHERDS, SHEPHERDESSES, *Pastoral* SCENES

Romantic pink is a constant—from the jewel tones of cranberry glass and fine stitches to pale tints of transferware village scenes and summer flowers. The color of spring buds and summer sunrises, pink connotes the delicacy of nature and shy blushes on dewy cheeks.

CRANBERRY GLASS, OLD *Silver*, HIGH SUMMER LIGHT

FERNS, *Flowers*, REMINDERS OF WOODS OR HIGHLANDS

OPPOSITE: *Stag-motif decoupaged plates flank a moody American Impressionist painting. Molding and finials detail a lime-oak bed purchased in London.* ABOVE LEFT: *A dignified stag painting reinforces the room's outdoors theme.* ABOVE RIGHT: *Plaid befits a room having overtones of the highlands.*

Transferware plates
detail the Gothic-style
window in the sunny
upstairs sitting room. A
classic Staffordshire
figurine provides the
base for the lamp on the
antique child-sized desk.

Floral motifs reflect the summerhouse's charming name, Rosecliffe Cottage. **RIGHT:** Adirondack furniture and a rustic picture frame impart a Maine woods tone to an attic bedroom decorated in a roses and fairies theme. **BELOW LEFT:** In the sunny yellow dine-in kitchen, the printed valance and curtains soften the Gothic-style detailing of the iron chandelier and the arched cabinet doors. **BELOW RIGHT:** A vintage quilt serves as a tablecloth on the harbor-facing dining porch.

FURNISHED WITH *Antique* PAINTED

LEFT: *A mix of antique wicker painted white and green relaxes the mood on the wide sitting porch. Ferns and blooming geraniums contribute to the old-fashioned charm. Child-sized chairs welcome young guests.* **RIGHT:** *The rose-motif fabric plays on the home's Rosecliffe name; cherries and strawberries reflect the summer theme.*

WICKER, THE PORCH IS THE *Classic* SUMMER LIVING ROOM

ROMANCE OF FLOWERS

*More expressive than the loveliest poem, flowers hint shyly at romantic
feelings or boldly proclaim passion. Cultures develop their own elaborate
flower languages, with emotions and meanings attached to varieties or colors.
Ephemeral flowers are destined to fade, but they are so beloved that blooms
and bouquets are saved, dried, or pressed, as remembrances of
sentimental times. From a bud in a toddler's hand to long-
stemmed roses, flowers are the language of
romance. Fill your home with
flowers and live the
romance every
day.*

When Romance Returns

A Romantic Home Tour

Narrow brick streets, hidden gardens, and beautifully restored homes, some predating the American Revolution, imbue Charleston, South Carolina, with the fabled romance of a small European city. A couple who met in the city as students never forgot Charleston's well-known charms and returned to transform a converted stable in the historic district into the home they always wanted.

Pinky and Pete Peters made it their quest to find a house in the downtown historic area. But no house ever seemed right until the day they walked into a former stable. The structure they found had been built in 1759 on the grounds of the Bradford Horry house next door. At some point in the 19th century, living quarters were added upstairs, and in 1913 the stable was converted into a livable two-story house.

"When we walked in, I knew this was the house," Pinky recalls. "I gave Pete a thumbs-up." Although it was obvious the house needed substantial work, the tall arches, originally used for carriages, the open architectural spaces, and the downstairs marble floors from an old Georgia courthouse entranced the couple. And the unusually high windows, while ensuring privacy from the busy street, provided light and views without heavy window treatments.

The house also appealed to Pinky's evolving taste for minimalism in decorating. "I loved the spaces and the marble; I hated to start adding things," she says. "The house dictated a lighter look than pieces we had in our previous homes."

In that vein, Pinky and her daughters, Meredith Dunnan, an interior designer, and Ashley Peters, an artist, worked with pale, neutral colors and edited the patterns and colors used in the couple's previous homes. This time, Pinky seriously pared down, eschewing English mahogany furniture and framed art for lighter painted and gilded Italian and French pieces. Arranged sparingly with minimal accessories, the traditional furniture takes on a sleek, more contemporary look.

Absent, too, are the collections from previous homes, replaced with a few select paintings by daughter Ashley, a Scottish portrait inherited from an aunt, and favorite English and French bronze figurative sculptures. Black accents, in lampshades, frames, and mats, pair with the dark bronzes to counterpoint the pale rooms and gilded furnishings.

Even the master suite is sparely furnished, with the bed and dressing table imparting a softer look without adornment. The striped slipcover for the vanity chair is one of the few patterned fabrics in the house. The ensuing ambience is relaxed and serene, Pinky's goal for her private retreat.

"Every time I open the door and walk in, I feel good," she says. "I like to live around things older than I am. And that's easy to do in Charleston."

The gold and black accents against a neutral background achieve a chic version of romantic style. Bronze figurines are the home's sole collection.

A gilded 19th-century bronze adds personality to the living room. RIGHT: *White fabrics and edited furnishings translate into an updated interpretation of traditional decorating.*

Animate PALE ROOMS AND *Gilded* FURNITURE.

Romantic *Style* is...

Ornate silver, aged English bronzes, and treasured pearls are all the more beautiful for signs of age, for the stories that surely accompany them. Who purchased the piece when it was new? Was it given in happiness? Or was it a reminder of a lovely, yet bittersweet, memory?

SILVER SHELLS, PEARLS, BRONZE *Figures* IN PENSIVE POSES

Associated with royalty, wealth, and splendor, touches of gold—in paint and embellishment—epitomize elegance and refinement. As the legend of King Midas teaches, gold is to be enjoyed in moderation. Sweet faces and spring wildflowers are lovelier than riches.

FACES AND
FLOWERS
FOREVER
Lovely

GILDED
WOOD,
Details
IN GOLD

LEFT: *Scrolls on the French baker's rack repeat the dramatic shape of the delicately scrolled iron chandelier.* **ABOVE RIGHT:** *An Italian table sets a convivial mood, while the tole tray creates a backdrop for decanters.* **BELOW RIGHT:** *Blue and white Chinese exportware and cobalt-blue goblets introduce vivid color.*

Black repeats in the Queen Anne-style armchair with painted detailing and the baby grand piano. The framed artwork is by Ashley Peters, Pinky Peters' daughter.

A ntiques, arranged
in edited, contemporary style, are as beautiful
as fine art in the restored home. ABOVE:
A Louis XVI-style armchair, upholstered in
black leather, contributes graceful curves
to the library. ABOVE RIGHT: The carved
French commode displays an antique
oil painting flanked by candlestick lamps.
Shades add touches of black. RIGHT: The
gilt-framed mirror reflects the foyer. A black
lacquered pedestal displays trailing ivy.

Plantation shutters ensure privacy without fabric in the master bedroom. Tapestry pillows introduce subtle pattern. The caned settee adds a touch of the tropics.

The oval mirror, flanked by candlestick lamps, imparts an old-fashioned touch to the graceful vanity table. The gathered, skirted slipcover adds a lively stripe to the scheme.

MAGIC AND MYSTERY

hat old black magic casts a spell of romance—an attraction as strong as it is unexplainable. Why someone loves a person, a place, or an object is more a matter of heart than head. Can anyone really explain what draws her or him to fulfill private desires? As the magnetic pull of opposites is the romance of myth and song, so, too, is the interplay of light and dark in decorating. Light-filled, pale interiors appear even more lustrous and delicate with the contrast of black accents. Create your own magic with touches of black and enjoy a sophisticated, grown-up romance.

TUSCANY INSPIRED VILLA

The charm of old-world architecture lives anew in a California home designed with the materials, care, and sun-warmed colors of the legendary Italian hill towns. Thick walls, covered loggias, and a secluded courtyard assure privacy. A mix of robust antiques, contemporary rugs, and finely crafted reproductions creates a relaxed interpretation of classic style.

Outside, bright sunshine bounces off the stucco walls and red tile roof. But inside the thick walls, rooms protected by a loggia and oriented to a private interior courtyard are cool and quiet. Mellow colors, natural tile floors, and rugged beams impart a rustic, yet refined, elegance.

The ambience of both architecture and interior design clearly echoes Tuscany, a region of Italy that translates well to dry and sunny California. The style is a shared passion for architects Drexel Patterson and Tony Crisafi and designer Constance Noah. "The house is romantic but in a robust way," says Constance. "There's nothing fragile or delicate about the architecture, the buildings, or the furnishings. My clients wanted a house they could enjoy with their friends and pets. They didn't want to worry about fragile objects."

In the mild climate, the enjoyment includes the loggia, which has a fireplace to encourage year-round outdoor sitting and dining. The courtyard beckons with its view, seen through generous French doors. Inside, the enjoyment is enhanced by the open kitchen with a curved island for casual entertaining with good friends.

Lighting, furnishings, and accessories reflect the old-world mood and enrich the shades of terra-cotta and ocher that dominate the restrained color scheme. Decorative trims and moldings, designed by the architects in the style of Italian hill towns, and custom-milled doors enrich the rooms with a timeless, classic quality.

Antique Italian iron chandeliers and decorative sconces light a collection of old rugs, antique furniture from Italy, and a few Country French pieces. Because the rooms are oriented to the private interior courtyard, window treatments are minimal. Rich fabrics are used judiciously as accents, such as the velvet portiere that frames the view to the dining room and its gracefully arched windows. Cotton chenilles, natural linens, and burlaps add texture without the distraction of pattern. European oil paintings and accessories, such as altar candlesticks and candelabra, porcelain lamps, Italian pottery, and antique leather-bound books, strengthen the Tuscan ambience.

The master suite, a private retreat with a fireplace and bath, opens to a small garden pool in the courtyard. The romance of the Old World resonates through rooms as ageless as they are beautiful.

Hand-painted detailing highlights the dining room arch and frames parchment-shade sconces flanking a 19th-century oil painting. The Italian-style table and chairs are reproductions.

The substantial silver
Louis XIV-style
candelabra features
ornate detailing and a
scrolled footed base. Such
elaborate pieces were
favorites of 19th-century
California wine barons.

MEMORABLE DINNERS *Past*

The gilded, carved French chandelier and decorative sconces enrich the dining room; a velvet portiere creates a sense of privacy. The sun-toned Jaipur rug was woven in India.

ABOVE LEFT: *The graceful lines of the carved shell chair complement the gilded harp in the music corner.* **BELOW LEFT:** *A painted Portuguese rush-seat side chair introduces a provincial touch.* **RIGHT:** *The tufted ottoman, mix of fabrics, and distressed finishes relax the large-scale living room furnishings and metal accents.*

Romantic Style is...

Romantic homes recast and interpret their own stories through design and decorative arts. The California Tuscan style alludes today, as in the 19th century, to the wine regions of Italy and France, where art, music, and hospitality were valued and shared in enticing settings.

CLASSIC ART AND EMBRACING *Cherubs*

The contrasts of rugged and refined, of strong and gentle, epitomize the fiery passion of romance. In robust country styles, delicate crystals hang from unadorned hand-forged iron chandeliers, and bronze farm roosters and rough stone are as appealing as cherubs and sculptures.

CRYSTALS THAT *Reflect* RUGGED IRON AND BRONZE.

CANDLES THAT *Glow* AND LIGHT THE NIGHT

New bar chairs, their design based on Italian style, invite friends to gather in the kitchen. Vintage lamps feature mica shades, often used in Arts and Crafts-style houses.

Mellow COLORS AND CARVED

French doors lead from the study library to the villa-style loggia, warmed by a fireplace. The elaborately carved desk recalls the heavy carved furniture of 19th-century California.

WOODS *Recall* OLD-WORLD ROMANCE.

arthy colors and distressed finishes impart age and character to a new home. **LEFT:** *French bistro chairs lighten the mood around a mosaic-and-stone table on the private terrace.* **BELOW LEFT:** *A subtle tone-on-tone wall treatment is an ideal backdrop for the painted cabinet in a guest bath.* **BELOW RIGHT:** *In the library, shield-back chairs pair with a pedestal chess table. The bamboo shade relaxes formal furnishings and gently softens the light and view of the loggia.*

Restyled and aged with antiquing glaze, the paneled bed with carved pineapple finials fits the scale of the guest suite. A mix of fabrics adds color and pattern to the comfortable setting.

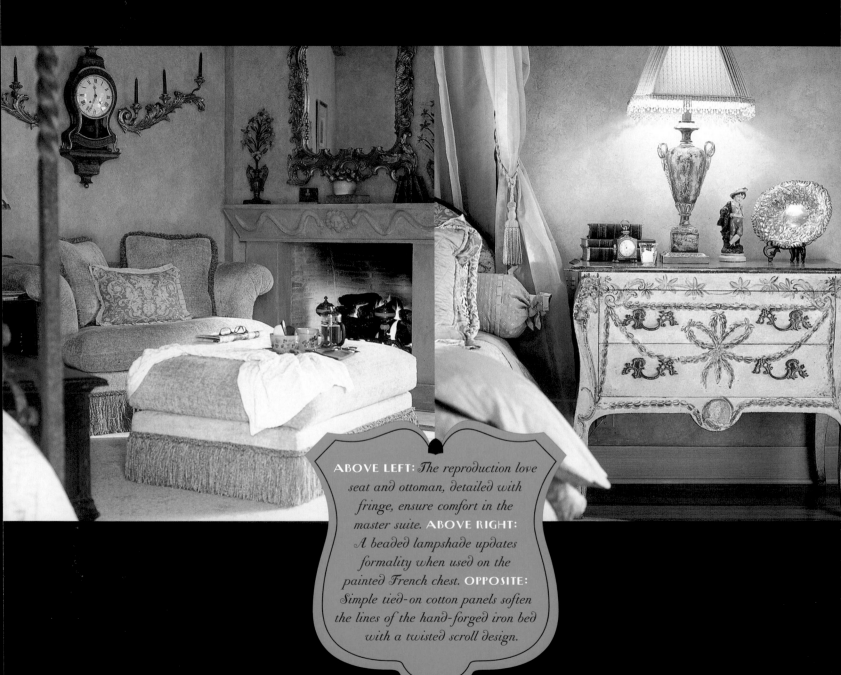

ABOVE LEFT: *The reproduction love seat and ottoman, detailed with fringe, ensure comfort in the master suite.* **ABOVE RIGHT:** *A beaded lampshade updates formality when used on the painted French chest.* **OPPOSITE:** *Simple tied-on cotton panels soften the lines of the hand-forged iron bed with a twisted scroll design.*

OPENS TO A *Private* POOL.

Architectural Embellishments

Elements of the past, old fragments given new life or reproduced from traditional motifs, warm and enrich. Architectural forms based on classic shapes, proportions, and materials recall ruins and fabled cultures. In sunny climates, architects and designers find inspiration in Italian classicism, a style with strong forms and earthy colors that twine back in time to villas and walled hill towns. New houses incorporate the old and artfully crafted new to achieve a style that calms and soothes. Here is the romance of strength, of beauty in the art of architecture.

Freshly
Edited
Opulence

A Romantic
home Tour

Using the pale colors inspired by an antique floral rug,

an artistic young mother works in the soft, gentle color palette that

refreshes a classic Tudor cottage in Minneapolis. Edited furnishings,

romantic chandeliers, and a pared-down approach to decorating add

a youthful spin to the project. A sunny Tuscan-inspired kitchen is

the perfect spot for informal family living and casual entertaining.

Marne Brooks dresses in chic contemporary style and wears sleek modern jewelry. Yet when she decorated the Minneapolis home she shares with her husband Dan and two young children, she gravitated to the softly romantic look of pale colors, muted patterns, and softly lit chandeliers. The colors of gently faded floral Aubusson rugs from France inspire her fresh, modern version of classic romantic style.

"It's not something I can explain," says Marne. "I'm drawn to traditional style and that influences my decorating. But I like a lot of space around pieces and a crispness to our rooms, definitely not clutter."

The Brook's 1906 Tudor-style house provides the background for her version of romantic, carefully edited traditional interiors. Sandy taupe walls with white trim are pale yet contrasting backdrops for the living room's white slipcovers and the darker wood tones in the dining room. Original art and carefully chosen architectural fragments, including some from the Paris flea market, star in the living room; accent pillows introduce touches of animal prints.

In the adjacent dining room, the home's most lavish and formal space, Marne worked out an eclectic scheme based on a custom pedestal table, pairs of chairs rather than a matching set, and a painted glass and wood sideboard from a Florida plantation. An antique chandelier, on a dimmer for mood, illuminates the sophisticated, distinctive furnishings. Lush draperies, made of velvet and tied with heavy cording, enrich and warm.

The romantic mood continues in the master bedroom and daughter Grace's bedroom. In the master bedroom, a crystal chandelier hangs to the side of the rococo-style painted headboard that recalls Italian and French furniture. The distressed finish artfully ages the bed while the hand-painted flowers are art for the room. Grace's room is a youthful take on sophisticated romance, with a smaller chandelier and toile fabrics setting the scene. The scalloped bed hanging, above the tufted headboard, creates an appealing coziness.

In a departure from the romance of paleness, Marne chose a rich Tuscan villa look for the kitchen and breakfast room. Golden toile curtains on wrought-iron rods launch the colorful decorating direction. The round table and black Windsor chairs invite friends to linger. "We wanted a house that we enjoy," Marne says. "Our rooms are for living."

LEFT: *Rosettes and vines decorate the fire screen in the living room.* **RIGHT:** *A mix of pretty, pale fabrics— slipcovers with flirty gathered skirts and accent pillows—imparts a fresh cottage feel to the living room, anchored by the antique floral rug. The unframed still life reiterates the youthful floral theme.*

AND FLORAL PAINTING *Whisper* OF SPRING IN THE GARDEN.

BELOW LEFT: *An architectural-fragment frame adds emphasis to a small portrait.*
BELOW RIGHT: *A mix of fabrics relaxes an otherwise formal room.*

PRETTY *Florals* AND A MIX OF FABRICS *Refresh* THE

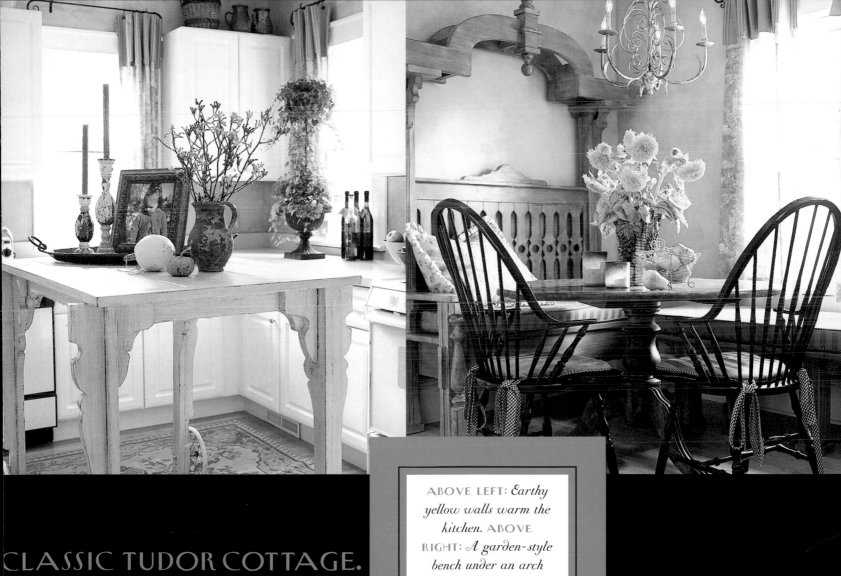

CLASSIC TUDOR COTTAGE.

ROMANTIC *Style* IS...

In the 19th century, painters, poets, and dreamers looked back on an idealized version of the Middle Ages to create the Romantic movement in the arts. The mix of metals and stone with exotic touches in mosaics and damasks continues to inspire devotees of romantic style.

ROSES, *Twining* IVY VINES, STEMS OF LILIES

Elements of the garden breathe life into romantic settings. Painted flowers bloom against a sophisticated black background; sweet rosebuds symbolize young innocence. Aged pedestal urns and footed cachepots are indoor gardens planted to flourish, whatever the season.

OLD-WORLD RICHES, *Cottage* SWEETNESS

SCROLLS, *Curves,* CRYSTALS, TINY BEADS

A *Curvy* FRENCH-STYLE HEADBOARD

SETS THE *Scene* FOR A ROMANTIC BEDROOM.

Finishing touches of tasseled braid and trim enrich the romantic mood of the master bedroom. The floral accent pillow on the chaise embellishes the neutral scheme.

BEDROOM *Pretty* ENOUGH FOR A PRINCESS.

OPPOSITE: *A scalloped bed hanging drapes the upholstered daybed in daughter Grace's bedroom. A diminutive crystal chandelier illuminates her whimsical painted table.* ABOVE LEFT: *A painted shelf holds childhood favorites.* ABOVE RIGHT: *Silvery paint transforms ball-and-claw tub feet into chic accents.*

CHANDELIERS OF CRYSTAL

nce designed to reflect candlelight, crystal chandeliers still light the night with their brilliant glow. Chandeliers ablaze with light and sparkle beckon guests into the foyer or illuminate dinner on a night of celebration. Converted from candlelight or gaslight, antique chandeliers are prized for their artistry and aged elegance. New chandeliers, their designs often emulating European prototypes, offer interpretations of old-world style. Chandeliers cast soft light in bedrooms and baths. Light up your own nights with the beautiful lighting of romance.

LINENS AND LACE

Lyrical in their delicate, ethereal beauty, antique European linens and

fragile handmade lace exemplify the painstaking skill of fine needlework

as they tell romantic stories from the past. Textiles from Asia and Africa are

equally stunning and express the artistry of rich cultures and the creativity of

their makers. In a Dallas home, collectors meld textiles from their years of

world travel into a sophisticated mix that is as exotic as it is romantic.

THE PEARL-ENCRUSTED *Chandelier Illuminates* A TABLE DRESSED FOR DINNER.

Charlotte Comer, a professional interior designer, gravitates to the unpretentious charm of old cottages for her own home. With her discerning eye, she and her husband, Ed, remodeled a circa-1914 two-story house as a backdrop for a soothing monochromatic palette and carefully edited furniture and finds, notably collected textiles. Although the remodeling is extensive, the goal was to add years to the vintage house, not subtract them.

"I didn't want to change so much that the house lost its sense of history, but I wanted to make this a home that says something about us," Charlotte says. This meant incorporating the details and textures of an older cottage in the living and dining room. To age and enrich the living room, Charlotte had beams installed and painted to resemble whitewashing, walls finished with a random texture, and stucco applied over the restyled fireplace.

In the dining room, gilded molding, a waxed wall finish, and a hand-painted ceiling meld into an elegant decorative canvas.

With the backgrounds in place, Charlotte then concentrated on simple color palettes emphasizing fabrics and textiles. In the living room, multiple layers of white fabric create Charlotte's desired monochromatic look. Varying textures, from matelassé to antique lace, add depth to the all-white scheme. Juxtapositions, such as a Kuba cloth from Africa hanging next to vintage lace curtain panels, personalize the setting. An antique Chinese bamboo vest hangs as art over the mantel.

Upstairs, linens and lace combine with wall cupboards for stylish display in the cozy sitting room for two and in the unabashedly romantic bedroom. In the sitting room, double café curtains are voile topped with a sheer table runner. Side panels are embroidered linen and lace tied with ribbons to the rod. Elegant white lace drapes the tea cart.

For the master bedroom, Charlotte tied panels of antique lace over voile on a drapery rod, slipcovered the chair in a matelassé bedspread, and found a spot for an antique dressing table and chest. For a finishing touch, she layered lace over the linen panels of the canopy bed and dressed the bed in vintage linens. The pristine white linens illustrate Charlotte's philosophy of furnishing her home with the things that appeal to her. "If you buy only what you love, you'll always find a place for it, and you'll have a home that feels right for you," she notes.

Sconces crafted from French ironwork pair with a pearl-trimmed chandelier to illuminate the metal-clad oval dining table. Painted chairs match the subtle wall finish.

ABOVE LEFT: *The spider web chair back echoes the shapes of the gilded mirrors. Curly bamboo adds an Asian touch.* **BELOW LEFT:** *An antique handkerchief drapes over a crystal goblet, emulating table settings in the tropics.* **RIGHT:** *Mirrored obelisks and a daybed in the recessed window introduce French accents.*

Matching handcrafted corner cabinets display a collection of white porcelains. Elevated on an aged pedestal, a tureen works as sculpture in the serene sitting room.

AND *Diffuses* WARM LIGHT.

Embroidered linen
and lace panels, tied
to the drapery rod with
satin ribbons, frame a
table runner above voile
cafe curtains. Antique
lace dresses the black tea
cart and serving tray.

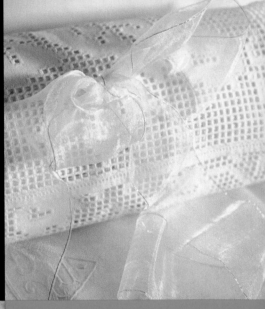

 ROMANTIC Style IS...

Exquisite details, from the embellishment of chandeliers, shades, and linens to richly set dining tables, clarify romantic style into an expression of artistic living. The touch of the hand in crochet and lace is cherished for the beauty it brings to everyday living.

SHIMMERING LIGHT AND EXOTIC *Jeweled* TOUCHES

Flower motifs, known as fleurettes in the French language, and the famous fleur-de-lis, stylized from the iris, denote the esteemed role of France in the decorative arts. Crystal and porcelain recall French contributions to the graceful arts of daily living and fine dining.

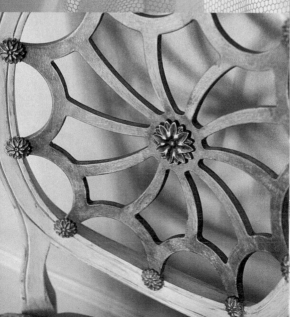

ROSES AND
CRYSTAL IN
Lush
SETTINGS

RUGGEDLY
Aged,
DELICATELY
REFINED

A Chinese vest crafted from bamboo hangs from an acrylic rod on the Country French-style chimney breast. The random-pattern wall finish with hints of gold mimics old plaster.

BACKGROUNDS FOR *Exotic* TEXTILES AND FINDS.

OPPOSITE: *Antique European linens and lace dress the French iron bed. Applied rosettes add detail to the decorative wall treatment.* ABOVE LEFT: *Country French-style cotton canopies and drapery panels contribute pattern to the guest room.* ABOVE RIGHT: *Lace-embellished beds flank the bamboo table and cloisonné lamp.*

146

SENSES IN *Luxurious* PRIVATE RETREATS.

TEXTILES
FROM NEAR AND FAR

he skills of hands, gentle and strong, create weaves, patterns, and embellishments indicative of their time, place, and maker. Such arts, often passed from mother to daughter, express how a culture nourishes and values beauty and craft. Everyday objects, from clothing to household linens, transcend the utilitarian to become true works of art. Collectors who love textiles furnish their homes with these treasures. Display your finds as art or as delicate window treatments. Set dining tables with vintage linens. Dress your bed for sweet dreams.

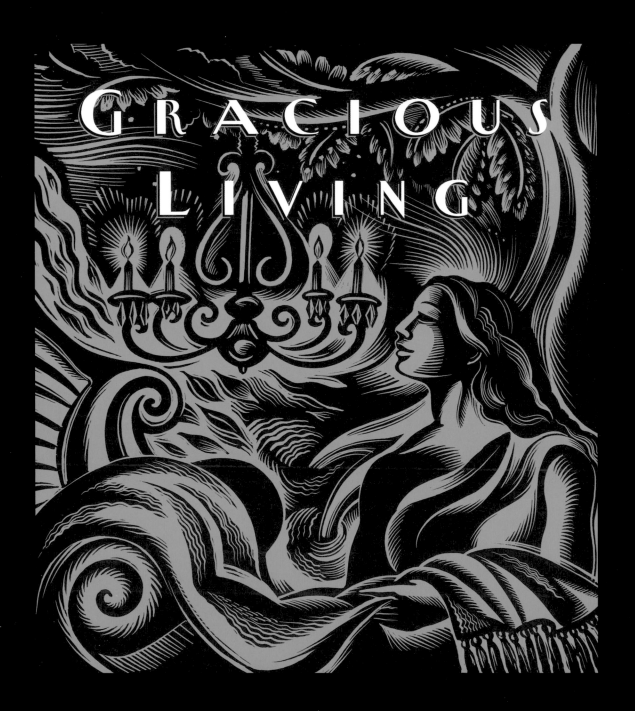

GRACIOUS LIVING

Soothing color palettes, soft lighting, unstructured window treatments, and comfortable upholstered furniture define rooms that invite relaxation. Art and accessories, chosen for their meaning and beauty, personalize without the chaos of clutter. Pale and ethereal or rich and jewel-hued, romantic rooms welcome all who enter their lovely confines.

WHITE REFRESHES AND POLISHES *Classic* STYLES

The pleasing scale and architectural detailing of pre-World War II homes, such as Tudor-style bungalows, appeal to many decorating enthusiasts. To lighten and brighten such classic houses and to offset dark woodwork, think large doses of creamy white and interesting mixes of upholstered furniture, antique or vintage furniture, and edited accessories. Instead of a sofa, try a space-saving daybed to avoid blocking light from windows. A carved table or tufted ottoman provides a striking alternative to the typical coffee table. Architectural fragments make dramatic art.

LEFT: *Silk draperies, hung at ceiling height to visually expand the living room, contrast with pale walls.*
ABOVE RIGHT: *The mantel displays ornate fragments.*
BELOW RIGHT: *A collection of mercury glass brightens a drop-leaf table.*

VICTORIAN STYLE *Meets* THE OLD WEST

The most intriguing romantic-style rooms emulate stage sets, depicting stories of fascinating times or places. The American West continues to live in myth and legend; so does the style created when affluent Westerners furnished their homes with the finest riches of the Victorian era. To create this look, think color-washed walls in the style of adobe, a vibrant mix of substantial Victorian-era furniture, and art and accessories from Europe, Mexico, and the American Southwest. Family photographs in ornate frames of the era personalize the heady mix of styles and textures.

LEFT: *A shapely blue velvet sofa, accented with decorative pillows, pairs with a tufted and fringed star-shaped ottoman.* RIGHT: *An antique table displays a crystal candelabra.*

A IRY COTTAGE AT THE *Seashore*

Poets and painters find inspiration in the ever-changing vistas of sand and sea. So do decorators who turn to seaside cottages and lighthouses for style ideas. Painted paneling and beaded board are natural backgrounds for a crisp theme, as are well-edited flea market finds refreshed with white and one unifying floral fabric. Art and accessories, displayed with a discerning eye, lean to the nautical with starfish and seashells neatly arranged. Lighthearted touches, such as a child-sized Adirondack chair, relax the scene.

OPPOSITE: *Seashells on a display board and a salvaged barber's pole serve as art and reminders of the ocean.*
BELOW: *The floor, sanded in an oversize diamond motif, anchors a living room that mixes an iris-print fabric and painted white tables.*

Welcome

DOUBLE LIFE FOR A *Romantic* HOME OFFICE

Who says a home office or study has to be all work—or that a combination living room and office must be strictly utilitarian? Think outside the boundaries and design a room for work and relaxing. To ensure that work isn't scattered around, start with concealed storage for the work space. If double doors aren't an option, add a decorative screen, often used in romantic-style rooms, to conceal workaday necessities from view. With business out of the way, make a statement with a painted floor, a beautiful window treatment, curvy furniture, soft lighting, and fine accessories.

LEFT: *A painted floor and handsome window treatment set the stage for a glamorous French-style sofa.* ABOVE: *Padded doors discreetly conceal the home office.*

BOTANICAL PRINTS *Enliven* THE LIVING ROOM

Traditional furniture takes on a romantic interpretation when floral fabrics and art with expansive white backdrops are part of the charming ambience. To achieve this look with ease, lighten upholstered sofas and chairs with a garden-flower print. Include pretty detailing such as scalloped edges, piping, and soft pleats that enhance the refined look. Arrange framed botanical art in a grid pattern or mix art with floral or botanical plates, such as majolica patterns. Opt for a sisal rug, glass coffee table, and stylized lamps. Fresh flowers bring botanical-inspired rooms to life.

A symmetrical furniture arrangement imposes order on the pretty floral scene. The mix of patterns adds variety. Staffordshire dogs and porcelain plates impart traditional touches.

SENSUOUS CURVES RECALL *Hollywood* GLAMOUR

If your idea of romance is the sleek interiors of the 1930s depicted in Hollywood films of the era, use the visual images for your own Art Moderne-inspired living room. Curvy furniture, crafted with minimal detailing and upholstered in solid fabrics, is a hallmark of the 20th-century look. In current interpretations, antiques and striking Asian pieces join the eclectic mix while sisal rugs contribute texture and a hint of the tropics without the distraction of pattern. Lushly gathered sheers, hung as drapery panels, hint at understated romance and coolly sophisticated glamour.

LEFT: *An innovative ottoman coffee table strikes a modern mood softened by lacy sheers.* ABOVE RIGHT: *The straight lines and stylized images of an Asian chest anchor a room of pale tints.* BELOW RIGHT: *Cool blues and greens contribute chic color.*

TUSCANY IN THE *Wine* COUNTRY

Romance is timeless, always elegant in a living room designed with the limestone fireplace, statuary, and fine library typical of grand Italian villas. Painted in mellow, sun-warmed hues, exquisitely detailed murals depict classical motifs in grand Baroque style; painted columns flank tall casement windows. Furnishings, including Italian chairs covered in leather, are scaled to the room's gracious proportions; velvets enrich the scheme. A pedestal library table, large urns, and a gilt-framed mirror complete the rich look.

Colors drawn from faded
frescoes add age to a
living room as romantic
as an Italian opera.
OPPOSITE: Armchairs
upholstered in leather
mix with a glass-top
pedestal library table.

GARDEN STYLE *Refreshes* COTTAGE CHARM

Cottage-style rooms are all the prettier when touches of the garden are invited inside. If this airy ambience is your idea of a romantic setting, look for white wicker and lightly distressed furniture as natural starting points. Add floral fabrics, new and old, for cushions and pillows. Search for special touches, such as a decorative screen or flea market needlework with a floral theme. For refined touches of charm, dress a floral lamp base with a shapely shade detailed with scalloped trim, and hang plates as art. Pottery urns, in clear pastels, add old-fashioned touches.

There is no Place Like Home

ABOVE: *Green and white, in checks and embroidery, contribute to the fresh-air feel.* LEFT: *A painted rattan table base melds with wicker enlivened by a mix of colorful fabrics.*

TRÈS French, TRÈS CHIC

The long-standing American love affair with French decorating is shown in evocative rooms with subtle finishes and casually elegant furnishings. The appeal of this look lies in understatement of color, fabric, and furnishings. To emphasize the French passion for architecture, add faux stone with marbleizing, a decorative painting technique that emulates veining. Romance the setting with sheer curtain panels hung from stylized iron rods and held in place with tiebacks. Finish with etchings or antique prints of classic architecture.

SUN-WARMED HUES *Embrace* A CALIFORNIA COTTAGE

Vintage pieces from the 1920s and 1930s offer the look of antiques without the price tags. To keep the look young and fun, pair tropical burnt-bamboo shades with floral drapery hung from a stylish iron rod. Look for 20th-century painted French and Italian tables and chests, often with gilt detailing, for a touch of affordable elegance. Such pieces are true flea-market and thrift-shop treasures. For art, hang canvases by Sunday painters, talented amateurs whose work is a favorite of thrift shop devotees. Mix in urns, silver trophies, and 20th-century art pottery for finishing touches.

LEFT: *A realistically painted fireplace sets the scheme for the warm and vibrant living room.*
RIGHT: *Roses in a silver loving cup grace a Florentine table detailed with gold leaf.*

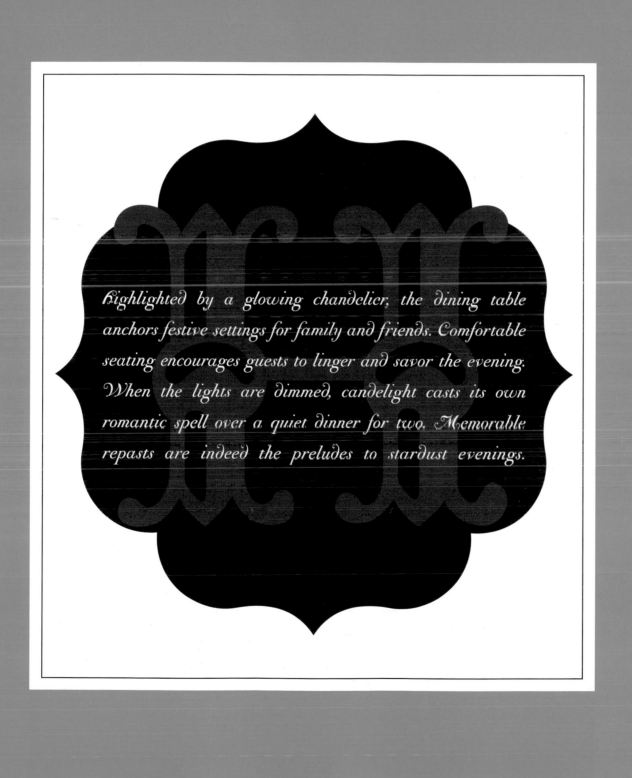

Highlighted by a glowing chandelier, the dining table anchors festive settings for family and friends. Comfortable seating encourages guests to linger and savor the evening. When the lights are dimmed, candelight casts its own romantic spell over a quiet dinner for two. Memorable repasts are indeed the preludes to stardust evenings.

SAVOR DINING *Amid* ROMANCE

Often the room where special memories are made, the dining room lends itself to many romantic interpretations. For a very pretty, dressed-up look, consider a soft blending of the popular English Country and European Continental styles created with sumptuous window treatments, lavish lighting, and period furniture. To set the color scheme, begin with a beautiful antique or vintage rug or even a rich fabric. Design window treatments, such as valances with side panels, that echo the tone. Include a less formal touch in a complementary fabric or accessory.

LEFT: *An ornate iron-and-crystal chandelier and sleek Louis XVI-style chairs introduce French accents.*
ABOVE: *The carved French fruitwood buffet serves as a sideboard.*

CHARMING GARDEN-STYLE Dining

Tiny dining rooms become romantic escapes when fabrics and furnishings are chosen with an eye to scale. As a start, hang a cupboard or shelf for collectibles. For a pretty, inviting room, choose a light, open print to repeat in simple window treatments and a tablecloth or table skirt. Look for vintage pieces such as painted wicker chairs to pair with a dining table and sideboard. Every room needs at least one unexpected touch; try installing a vintage crystal chandelier, but update it with trimmed fabric- or paper-covered shades.

OPPOSITE: *Floral motifs detail the shelf above the oil painting found at a flea market. The dry sink is used as a small-scale server.*
BELOW: *An unframed sunflower painting, a playful reference to the garden outside, relaxes the chandelier.*

OUTDOOR ELEMENTS *Recall* THE GARDEN

Script a scene of fresh-air romance with a dining room that welcomes pretty picturesque garden ornaments. As a backdrop for this appealing venue, work in shades of fresh green and white for walls and fabrics used for softly draped window treatments, slipcovers, and a table skirt. Add pieces such as garden gates, chairs, a bench, statuary, and plants that evoke the mood of the civilized outdoors. Incorporate overhead lighting in a lantern style appropriate to the indoor-outdoor theme and include green plants to create the feel of a conservatory.

LEFT: *Ivy twines up the decorative ironwork in a garden-style dining room embellished with wallpaper panels.* **RIGHT:** *A classic bust on a pedestal contributes a refined touch.*

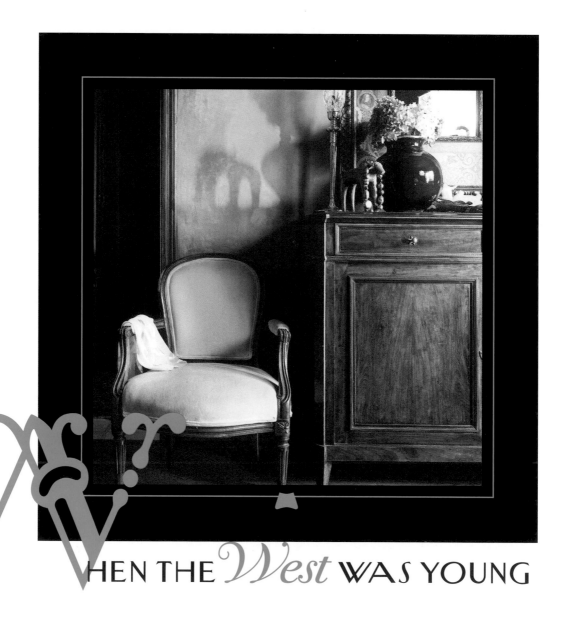

WHEN THE West WAS YOUNG

The romance of the American Southwest continues to capture the imaginations of historians, writers, and decorators. On the great ranches, families furnished their homes with a mix of refined furnishings and art imported from the East, and locally made furniture and crafts influenced by Mexican and Native American cultures. To create rooms that evoke this adventurous Western spirit, start with richly colored walls that emulate faded adobe; then add traditional 19th-century furniture in the jewel velvets of the period.

FRESH FLORALS IMPART *Cottage* ROMANCE

Think country cottages for a decorating look that is youthful and refreshing. Begin your scheme with pretty, old-fashioned wallpaper in shades of pink and cream. Look for traditional patterns such as roses or peonies, with creamy, open backgrounds. Treat windows lightly with sheers, shutters, or simple white blinds as needed for privacy. Mix chairs, perhaps combining delicately painted wood and natural wicker, to create a dining room that serves your needs. Illuminate the scene with an antique or reproduction chandelier in an aged finish that works with vintage style.

LEFT: *Hand-painted flowers on the chairs replicate the full bouquets on the wallpaper.* ABOVE RIGHT: *Seashells fill milk glass elevated on a cake stand.* BELOW RIGHT: *A sepia-toned family photograph captures a sunny day at the beach.*

AGED ELEGANCE MIXES *Shabby* WITH CHIC

Growing more beautiful with the years, the gently aging, still-elegant houses of fabled cities fascinate lovers of the exotic and the romantic. To emulate the layers of time, decorators turn to artful wall finishes and sun-bleached colors as backdrops. Refined furniture, ornate mirrors, regal chandeliers, and art stand out against the rugged, worn walls and ceiling. For this version of faded romance, start with an aged or washed wall finish and add sculptural furniture such as lacquered antique or reproduction neoclassical-style pieces in black and gold.

LEFT: *Created to recall layers of paint, the wall finish adds the patina of age to a new dining room.* **RIGHT:** *Silver flatware and jewel-tone glass add playful touches to a chandelier.*

HE AGE OF *Innocence* RETURNS

Cool colors and lustrous silk fabrics transform traditional furnishings into sophisticated and chic dining rooms. In this carefully edited version of romance, restraint is the key with shades of white, cream, and taupe ensuring serene backdrops for the finely detailed furnishings and art. Color, when it is used, appears in tiny touches of equally cool greens and purples. To decorate in this spirit, practice the art of restraint when choosing wall colors, furniture, and fabrics. But break the rules when color unexpectedly beckons.

OPPOSITE: *Botanical prints hang above a demi-lune server in the pristine dining room.* BELOW: *A delicate floral print contributes color to the monochromatic scheme.*

DRAMATIZE A DINING ROOM FOR *Grown*-UP ROMANCE

For a boldly beautiful setting, emphasize the contrasts of light and dark and rugged and refined. In a rustic setting of dark woods, or a dining room painted in deep tones, play on the creative tension with pale solid fabrics, white furniture, and glass. Work with large-scale, sculptural furnishings, which imbue a room with instant drama. Repeat the generous scale in window treatments, using floor-length draperies paired with a decorative valance or hung in lush ballgown style from an iron rod. Add a noteworthy chandelier to highlight the drama below.

White paint and upholstery update Queen Anne-style dining chairs while matching fabric works equal magic for traditional wing chairs. Crystal beads sensuously drape the chandelier.

NATURE RELAXES A *Setting* OF TREASURED FINDS

In keeping with the trend toward pared-down decorating, romantic style takes a youthful, contemporary direction with edited furnishings and personal touches. Create the scene with a two-toned paint treatment (a casual interpretation of wainscoting) and sleek, woven rattan chairs. Add large-scale drama with an ornate mirror or framed art, propped rather than hung for a casual effect. Shop antiques and thrift stores for brown and cream plates as a neutral version of transferware. In the same free spirit, relax a dressy iron chandelier with a rustic vine wreath.

LEFT: *A painted
sideboard proves the
perfect display for
aged urns flanking
a gilt-framed mirror.*
ABOVE: *A chaise
longue turns a corner
into a private retreat.*

ROMANTIC
BEDROOMS

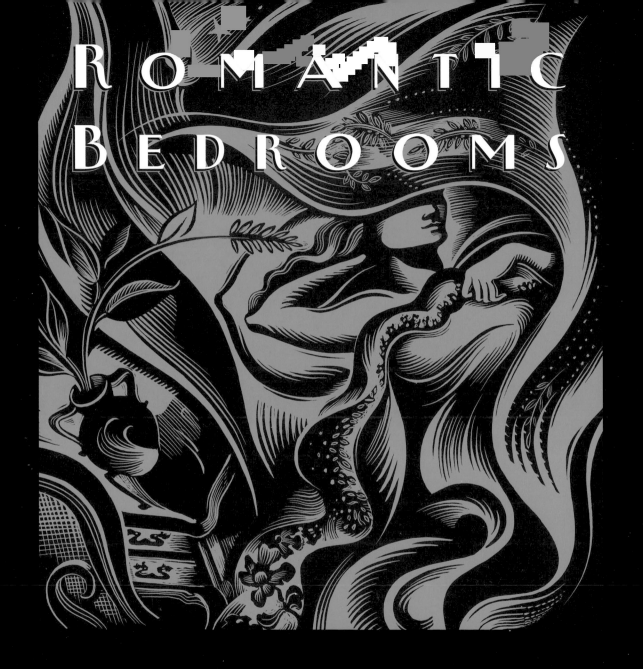

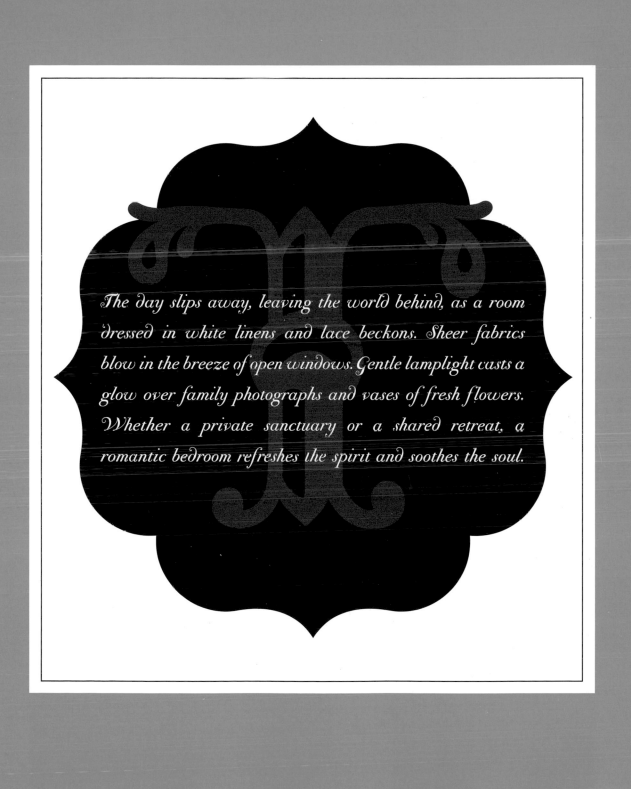

The day slips away, leaving the world behind, as a room dressed in white linens and lace beckons. Sheer fabrics blow in the breeze of open windows. Gentle lamplight casts a glow over family photographs and vases of fresh flowers. Whether a private sanctuary or a shared retreat, a romantic bedroom refreshes the spirit and soothes the soul.

GLORIOUS *Gold* AND SOFT WHITE

A gold and white scheme imbues a room with a tone of understated beauty and elegance appropriate for the most romantic of bedrooms. The lavishly dressed French bed, writing table, and chic Louis XVI-style side chair set the stylish direction; the tufted ottoman contributes an element of comfort. Accessories such as the beautifully detailed mirror and the shapely fire screen complete the look. Sconces with delicate shades and an urn pedestal lamp provide lighting; gentle swags and side panels soften the ambience.

LEFT: *Gold and black accents enhance the French-inspired bedroom.* **ABOVE:** *A calligraphy fabric updates the Louis XVI-style side chair; roses fill a conical vase.*

EDWARDIAN RECALLED

Elegance

Lovers of jewel tones and romance find a pleasing decorating inspiration in the Edwardian period, the era following the Victorian era. Based on a time when England was a world power and ruled the seas, the style incorporates deep color, fine fabrics, traditional furniture and art—and exotic touches from the far reaches of the British Empire. Damask-patterned wallpaper, popular in England, contrasts with the tropical sisal rug, white linens, and Asian cabinet and artifacts. The metal table recalls the portable campaign furniture that traveled with English officers.

LEFT: *Forest-green damask patterned wallpaper transforms a small bedroom into a restful retreat.* ABOVE RIGHT: *The lacquered chest and mask introduce Asian influences.* BELOW RIGHT: *A folding table provides a pleasant spot for work.*

EXOTIC *Style* WELCOMES GUESTS

East-meets-West decorating incorporates stylish furnishings to evoke the mood of far-away lands and travels. In this sophisticated, worldly design, gold and black accents bridge cultures stylishly to meld divergent looks and furnishings. To create harmony in such a wide-ranging version of romance, start with a strong focal point, such as an exotic bed, dramatic fabric, or striking artwork. Choose a background that amplifies without overpowering. Look for shapely lamps and accessories that enhance the well-traveled look.

OPPOSITE: *Detailed in golden paint, the chest displays barley-twist lamps with sleek black shades.* BELOW: *Trimmed in bamboo, the lavish decoupaged bed dressed in linens and silk conjures up images of Asian gardens. Walls are hand-painted.*

PRETTY FLOWERS IN A *Country* COTTAGE

Vintage linens and lace soften the scene, teaming with white-painted furniture and delicate florals to create rooms of romance and charm. To achieve this look, set the stage with shapely furniture pieces, including a four-poster bed and dressing table. If necessary, paint darkly stained or already-painted pieces in a soft white shade and slipcover upholstered pieces to blend with the scheme. Shop flea markets and antiques stores as well as linen shops to dress the bed, windows, and vanity. Accent with floral touches in rugs and fabrics for a spring-fresh finish.

LEFT: *An ornate mirror reflects the scene in a pretty linen-and-lace bedroom. Fabric covers swing-arm lamps.*
ABOVE: *Cutwork embroidery adorns the dressing table lamp.*

COOL SERENITY *Invites* RESTFUL DREAMS

Sophisticated romantic style creates bedrooms as sanctuaries from the cares of the day. Such a room naturally evokes the chic style of a Paris apartment with a mix of soft colors, fine furnishings, and a few well-chosen accessories. In a room where comfort reigns supreme, think of soothing shades of blues enlivened by subtle golden accents. Add extra touches, such as a handsome bench and a throw, to ensure both the look and feel of worldly comforts.

ABOVE: *Pinch-pleat draperies give tailored balance to a room of European-style furnishings.* OPPOSITE: *A striped shade provides a tailored finish for the glass urn lamp.*

YOUTHFUL TAKE ON *Old*-FASHIONED STYLE

Rely on fabric and accessories to transform vintage furniture from a thrift shop or the family attic into romantic bedroom pieces. To soften a metal or wood bed, hang a sheer fabric from the ceiling mosquito net-style and gently drape it over the headboard. Dress the bed in a mix of florals and lacy linens, adding a soft throw to complete the scene. Hang floral draperies, sheer panels, or classic curtains. Add interesting and gently aged accessories such as urns, small sculptures, or an old clock. Bring in outdoor freshness by displaying a green plant or two.

LEFT: *A fringed swag softens pinch-pleat draperies in a floral bedroom.* ABOVE: *Gauzy sheers emulate tropical mosquito netting to create an exotic look of romance.*

SOFT FABRICS, *Beautiful* FABRICATIONS

Open the door to a romantic bedroom decorated with shapely furniture and soft, sensuous fabrics. To create such an enticing look, begin your scheme with a four-poster bed with the requisite bed hangings. Sheer fabrics refine and soften metal or wood beds and add an element of visual privacy in a larger bedroom. Choose a tufted, upholstered ottoman, rather than a bench, for cushy comfort. Likewise, opt for a writing table or desk with curvy legs, and slipcover the desk chair with a graceful floor-length skirt. A small footstool adds a refined accent.

A patterned carpet grounds a lovely bedroom with the effect of a field of flowers. An antique chest serves as a nightstand, while lamps cast soft light over the pale scheme.

MIRRORS RECALL 1930s *Glamour*

Crafted in elaborate patterns, silvery Venetian mirrors grace rooms with old-world charm. The prized mirrors translate into etched mirrored valances, imparting an almost magical touch of big-city glamour. In keeping with the fantasy theme, a starburst candle chandelier illuminates a stylized daybed featuring handblown colored glass finials and feet; an aged mirror reflects the scene. Sheer fabrics, from flowing draperies trimmed with beads to a pleated gossamer slipcover, soften without concealing.

OPPOSITE: *A bronze candelabra imparts an appropriate theatrical touch to a bedroom bathed in cool, mirrored light.* BELOW: *A harlequin-patterned coverlet provides a subtle reminder of the theatrical inspirations for this glamorous retreat.*

GOLDEN WOOD AND *Swedish* SIMPLICITY

Pale colors and stylized nature-inspired motifs imbue country versions of Scandinavian design with sophistication as well as charm. Classic furniture pieces and simple window treatments stand out in well-edited rooms where form rules and clutter retreats. For a romantic take on this appealing style, choose a shapely bed, such as the classic sleigh bed, and dress it in white cottons. Paint or bleach wood floors to reflect light and hand-paint stylized vines and leaves on pale walls. Hang tabbed sheers at the windows to blow gently in the summer breeze.

LEFT: *Sheer fabric drapery gracefully frames the decorative wall-mounted bracket.* ABOVE RIGHT: *A gilt mirror reflects light in the Swedish-style room.* BELOW RIGHT: *Pegs mounted inside the painted wall frame are attractive as well as useful.*

Romantic Resources

ALABAMA

Brass Bed Interiors & Design: 2813 18th St. S., Homewood, AL 35209; 205/879-5474

Christine's: 2822 Petticoat Ln., Mt. Brook, AL 35223; 205/871-8297

Christine's Across the Street: 2423 Canterbury Rd., Mt. Brook, AL 35223; 205/871-6611

Sweet Peas: 2829 Linden Ave, Homewood, AL 35209; 205/879-3839

White Flowers Gallery: 2824 Cahaba Rd., Mt. Brook, AL 35223; 205/871-4640

ARKANSAS

Cabbage Rose: 5701 Kavanaugh Blvd., Little Rock, AR 72207; 501/664-4042

Marshall Clements: 1509 Rebsamen Park Rd., Little Rock, AR 72202; 501/663-1828

Pflugrad's Antiques: 5624 R St. Little Rock, AR 72207; 501/661-0188

CALFORNIA

Bed and Breakfast—Il Nido Nel Giardino: 354 E. Napa St., Sonoma, CA 95476; 707/939-0159; www.il-nido.com

Alabaster, Treasures for the Home: 597 Hayes St., San Francisco, CA 94102; 415/558-0482; www.alabastersf.com

Bountiful: 1335 Abbot Kinney Blvd., Venice, CA 90291; 310/450-3620; www.bountiful-online.com

Chelsea Antiques: 148 Petaluma Blvd. N., Petaluma, CA 94952; 707/763-7686

Drum & Company: 115 Main St., Saint Helena, CA 94574; 707/963-0919

Habité: 963 Harrison St., San Francisco, CA 94107; 415/543-3315; www.habite.com

Kevin Simon: 1358 Abbot Kinney Blvd., Venice, CA 90291; 310/392-4630; www.kevinsimonclothing.com

Living Green Plantscape Design: Three Henry Adams St., San Francisco, CA 94103; 415/864-2251

Nest: 2300 Fillmore St., San Francisco, CA 94115; 415/292-6199 and 2340 Polk St., San Francisco, CA 94109; 415/292-6198

Pullman & Co.: 108 Throckmorton Ave., Mill Valley, CA 94941; 415/383-0847

Renaissance: 124 W. Napa St., Sonoma, CA 95476; 707/935-8223

Sienna: 119 Petaluma Blvd. N., Petaluma, CA 94952; 707/763-6088

Sue Fisher King: 3067 Sacramento St., San Francisco, CA 94115; 415/922-7276

Summer House: 1833 Fourth St., Berkeley, CA 94710; 510/549-9914 and 21 Throckmorton Ave., Mill Valley, CA 94941; 415/383-6695

The Collective of San Anselmo: 316 Sir Francis Drake Blvd., San Anselmo, CA 94960; 415/453-6373

Yard Art: 2188½ Sutter St. at Pierce, San Francisco, CA 94115; 415/346-6002; www.yardartsf.com

COLORADO

Cadeaux: 232 West Colorado Ave., Telluride, CO 81435; 970/728-2055

CONNECTICUT

Cadeaux: 250 Greenwich Ave., Greenwich, CT 06830; 203/629-8595; www.cadeauxart.com

Clementine Inc.: 117 Main St., Westport, CT 06880; 203/227-4866

Devonshire, The English Garden Shop: 1 Wilton Rd. , Westport, CT 06880; 203/454-0648

East of West: 1603 Post Rd. Fairfield, CT 06430; 203/256-8298

Green: 103 Greenwich Ave., Greenwich, CT 06830; 203/863-9120

Hoagland's of Greenwich: 175 Greenwich Ave., Greenwich, CT 06830; 203/869-2127

Lillian August Collection: 17 Main St., Westport, CT 06880; 203/454-1775

Lynnens Inc.: 278 Greenwich Ave., Greenwich, CT 06830; 203/629-3659; www.lynnens.com

Parc Monceau: 1375 Post Rd. East, Westport, CT 06880; 203/319-0001; www.parcmonceau .com

Prince of Wales: 1032 and 1046 Post Rd. East, Westport, CT 06880; 203/454-2335

Private Quarters: 2600 Post Rd., Southport, CT 06490; 203/254-2300

Prosperity Interiors: 1330 Post Rd. East, Westport, CT 06880; 203/255-2734; www.prosperityinteriors.com

Saybrook Country Barn: Two Main St., Old Saybrook, CT 06475; 860/388-0891, www.saybrookcountrybarn.com

Souleiado: 190 Main St., Westport, CT 06880; 203/227-0704 and 14 Main St., Chester, CT 06412; 860/526-1480

Stuart Collection: 5 Post Rd. West, Westport, CT 06880; 203/221-7102

United House Wrecking: 535 Hope St., Stamford, CT 06906-1300; 203/348-5371, www.unitedhousewrecking.com

Uproar Home: 36 Elm Street, Westport, CT 06880; 203/221-9210; www.uproarhome.com

FLORIDA

Antique European Linens: 14 N. Palafox St., Pensacola, FL 32501; 850-432-4777; www.antiqueeuropeanlinens.com

GEORGIA

Acquisitions: 631 Miami Circle N.E., Atlanta, GA 30324; 404/261-2478 and 345 Peachtree Hills Ave. N.E., Atlanta, GA 30305; 404/237-8414

Addington-Osborne Ltd.: 3226 Roswell Rd. N.W., Atlanta, GA 30305; 404/240-0291

Boxwoods Gardens & Gifts Inc.: 100 E. Andrews Dr. N.W., Atlanta, GA 30305; 404/233-3400

Erika Reade Ltd.: 3732 Roswell Rd. N.W., Atlanta, GA 30342; 404/233-3857

Gado Gado Inc.: 549 Amsterdam Ave. N.E., #4, Atlanta, GA 30306; 404/885-1818; www.gadogado.com

Previews Interiors & Antiques: 4524 Forsyth Rd., #101, Macon, GA 31210; 800/456-1086; www.previewsinteriors.com

Provenance Antiques & Area Rugs: 1157 Foster St. N.W., Atlanta, GA 30318; 404/351-1217

ILLINOIS

Bedside Manor: 38 S. Garfield Ave., Hinsdale, IL 60521; 630/655-0497 or 929 Green Bay Rd., Winnetka, IL, 60093; 847/441-0969 or 2056 N. Halsted St., Chicago, IL, 60614; 773/404-2020; www.bedsidemanorltd.com

Faded Rose: 1017 W. Armitage Ave., Chicago, IL 60614; 773/281-8161

Jayson Home: 1911 N. Clybourn Ave., Chicago, IL 60614; 773/525-3100

Jayson Garden: 1885 N. Clybourn Ave., Chicago, IL 60614; 773/248-8180

Les Tissus Colbert: 207 W. State St., Geneva, IL 60134; 630/232-9940

Pariscope: 22 N. Third St., Geneva, IL 60134; 630/232-1600

Willow Design: 115 S. Batavia Ave., Batavia, IL 60510; 630/482-9233

IOWA

C'est La Vie: 114 5th St., West Des Moines, IA 50265; 515/255-2400; fax: 515/255-2700

Sisters Garden: 4895 Hwy 1 S.W., Kalona, IA 52247; 319/683-2046

LOUISIANA

Ann Connelly Fine Art: 2347 Christian St., Baton Rouge, LA 70808; 225/336-0204; fax: 225/336-0207

Au Vieux Paris Antiques: 1040 Henri Penne Rd., Breaux Bridge, LA 70517; 337/332-2852; fax: 337/332-6053; www.auvieuxparisantiques.com

Bremermann Designs: 3943 Magazine St., New Orleans, LA 70115; 504/891-7763

Bush Antiques: 2109 Magazine St., New Orleans, LA 70130; 504/581-3518; fax: 504/581-6889; www.bushantiques.com

Lucullus: 610 Chartres St., New Orleans, LA 70130; 504/528-9620 and 3932 Magazine St., New Orleans, LA 70115; 504/894-0500

Mac Maison: 3963 Magazine St., New Orleans, LA 70115; 504/891-2863

Mario Villa Gallery: 3908 Magazine St., New Orleans, LA 70115; 504/895-8731; www.mariovillagallery.com

MAINE

The Romantic Room: Rockend and Neighborhood Rds., Northeast Harbor, ME 04662; 207/276-4005 and Main St., Northeast Harbor, ME 04662; 207/276-4006

MARYLAND

Edward & Edward: 35 S. Carroll St., Frederick, MD 21701; 301/695-9674,

Urban Country Designs Ltd.: 7801 Woodmont Ave., Bethesda, MD 20814; 301/654-0500

Chevy Chase Antiques Galleria: 5221 Wisconsin Ave. N.W., Washington, D.C. 20015; 202/364-0842

MINNESOTA

Casabella: 5027 France Ave. S., Edina, MN 55410; 612/927-4875,

Patina: 1009 W. Franklin Ave., Minneapolis, MN 55405; 612/821-9315 and 2305 18th Ave. N.E., Minneapolis, MN 55418; 612/788-8933 and 5001 Bryant Ave. S., Minneapolis, MN 55419; 612/821-9315

Paris Flea Market: 5005 France Ave. S., Minneapolis, MN 55410; 612/928-9923

Pure Bliss: 211 East Main St., Anoka, MN 55303; 763/323-8160

Wigglestix Collection: 402 N. Main St., Stillwater, MN 55082; 651/439-1098; www.wigglestix.com

Camrose Hill Flower Shop: 233 S. 2nd St., Stillwater, MN 55082; 651/351-9631; www.camrosehillflowers.com

Lagos Hill: 867 Grand Ave., St. Paul, MN 55105; 651/224-6644

MISSISSIPPI

The Elephant's Ear: 3110 Old Canton Road, Jackson, MS 39216; 601/982-5140; www.elephantsear.com

NEW HAMPSHIRE

Garnet Hill, Inc.: 231 Main St., Franconia, NH 03580; 800/870-3513; www.garnethill.com

NEW YORK

The Apartment: 101 Crosby St., New York, NY, 10012; 212/219-3661

Moss: 146 Greene St., New York, NY 10012; 212/226-2190; www.mossonline.com

Modern Stone Age: 54 Greene St., New York, NY 10013; 212/219-0383

Coconut Company: 131 Greene St., New York, NY 10012; 212/539-1940

Peacock Alley: 334 E. 59th St, New York, NY 10022; 212/751-7005

ABC Carpet and Home: 888 Broadway, 4th Fl., New York, NY 10003; 212-473-3000

Chelsea Garden Center: 435 Hudson St., New York, NY 10014; 212/727-7100

Interieurs: 151 Franklin St., New York, NY 10013; 212/343-0800

Leron: 750 Madison Ave., New York, NY 10021, 800/954-6369; 212/753-6700; www.leron.com

Frette: 799 Madison Ave., New York, NY 10021; 212/988-5221, www.frette.com

Pratesi Linens: 829 Madison Ave., New York, NY 10021; 212/288-2315

Pierre Deux Fabrics: 870 Madison Avenue, New York, NY 10021; 212/570-9343; wwwpierredeux.com

White On White: 888 Lexington Ave., New York, NY 10021; 212/288-0909

Uproar Home: 121 Greene St., New York, NY 10012; 212/614-8580

The Finished Room: 1027 Lexington Ave., New York, NY 10021; 212/717-7626

Palumbo: 972 Lexington Ave., New York, NY 10021; 212/734-7630; www.palumbogallery.com

AR Breizh Antiques: 37-A Bedford St., New York, NY 10014; 212/243-8683

French General: 35 Crosby St., New York, NY 10013; 212/343-7474; www.frenchgeneral.com

Prince of Wales: 303 Central Park Avenue, Scarsdale, NY 10583; 914/686-3108

TEXAS

Ceylon et Cie: 1500 Market Center Blvd., Dallas, TX 75207; 214-742-7632

Eccentricities: 1921 Westheimer Rd., Houston, TX 77098; 713/523-1921

Horchow Finale: 3046 Mockingbird Lane, Dallas, TX 75205; 214/750-0308 and 3400 Preston Road, #210, Plano, TX 75093; 972/519-5406

Kay O'Toole Antiques and Linens Unlimited: River Oaks Shopping Center, 1992 West Gray, Houston, TX 77019; 713/529-4446

Longoria Collection: 1101-02 Uptown Park Blvd., Houston, TX 77056; 713/621-4241

Minton-Corley Collection: 2623 White Settlement Rd., Fort Worth, TX 76107; 817/332-8993

Olivine: 6586 Woodway Dr., Houston, TX 77057; 713/463-7308

Peacock Alley: 3210 Armstrong Ave., Dallas, TX 75205; 800/652-3818; www.peacockalley.com

Peacock Alley Outlet: 13720 Midway Rd., Ste. 203, Dallas, TX 75244; 972/490-3998

Rue No. 1: 6701 Snider Plaza, Dallas, TX 75205; 214/265-0900

Sanctuary: Preston Center Plaza, 4020 Villanova, Dallas, TX 75225; 214-739-0767

Sticks and Stones Garden Market: 5016 Miller Ave., Dallas, TX 75206; 214-824-7277

The Sitting Room/Ginger Barber Design Inc.: 2121 Woodhead, Houston, TX 77019; 713/523-1932; fax: 713/523-1929; www.thesittingroom.net

Victoria's Fine Linens: 1801-1B Post Oak Blvd., Houston, TX 77056; 713/840-8558

Watkins Culver Gardner: 2308 Bissonnet St., Houston, TX 77005; 713/529-0597

Yves Delorme: 4270 Oak Lawn, Dallas, TX 75219; 214-526-2955

VIRGINIA

Beekeeper's Cottage: 42350 Lucketts Rd, Leesburg, VA 20176; 703/771-9006 and 43738 Hay Rd., Ashburn, VA 20147; 703/726-9411

WASHINGTON, DC

Catharine Roberts Antiques: 1657 Wisconsin Ave. N.W., Washington, DC 20007; 202/338-7410

D. Strickland Antiques: 1653 Wisconsin Ave. N.W., Washington, DC 20007; 202/333-1653

David Bell Antiques: 1655 Wisconsin Ave. N.W., Washington, DC 20007; 202/965-2355

Marston Luce: 1314 21st St. N.W., Washington, DC 20036-1504; 202/775-9460

Moss & Co.: 1657 Wisconsin Ave. N.W., Washington, DC 20007; 202/337-0540

CATALOGS

Anthropologie: 800/309-2500; www.anthropologie.com

Ballard Designs: to order a catalog, 800/367-2775; for customer service, 800/367-2810; www.ballarddesigns.com

Exposures: 800/572-5750; www.exposuresonline.com

Horchow Home: 800/456-7000; www.horchow.com

Yves Delorme: to request a catalog, find store locations, or obtain product information, www.yvesdelorme.com

MONTREAL, CANADA

Antiquité Décoration Art: 1838 rue Notre Dame West, Montreal, Quebec H3J 1M5, Canada; 514/937-2440

DMC Antiquities: 1874 rue Notre Dame West, Montreal, Quebec H3J 1M6, Canada; 514/931-6722

Les Village des Antiquaries: 1708 Notre Dame West, Montreal, Quebec H3J 1M3 Canada; 514/931-5121

Passé Présent: 320 rue St. Paul West, Montreal, Quebec H2Y 2A3, Canada; 514/499-0062; fax: 514/499-3056, e-mail: elleiram@caramail.com

Pierre St. Jacques Antiquaire: 2507 rue Notre Dame West, Montreal, Quebec H3J 1N6, Canada; 514/933-9293

PARIS, FRANCE

Aux Armes de Furstenberg: 1, rue de Furstenberg, Paris; 01 43 29 79 51

Blanc d'Ivoire: 4, rue Jacob, 75006 Paris; 01 46 33 34 29

Christian Tortu: 6, Carrefour de l'Odéon, 75006 Paris; 01 43 26 92 56

Comoglio Paris: 22, rue Jacob 18th, 75006 Paris; 01 43 54 65 86

Flamant Home Interiors: 8, rue de Furstenberg, 75006 Paris; 01 56 24 13 26

Librairie Flammarion: La Maison Rustique, 26, rue Jacob, 75006 Paris; 01 42 34 96 60

Olaria: 30, rue Jacob, 75006 Paris; 01 43 25 27 21

Pierre Frey: 7, rue Jacob, 75006 Paris; 01 43 26 82 61

Yveline: 4, rue de Furstenberg 75006 Paris, 01 43 26 56 91

Index

A

Accessories, 12, 24–26, 41, 90–91
  California cottage-style, 170
  classical statues, 179
  family treasures, 52, 56, 58
  floral-themed, 143
  French-style, 44
  mixed materials in, 58–59, 126
  nautical, 156, 157
  old-world-style, 102, 126–127
  Scottish Highlands-style, 74–75
  softening furniture with, 204
  Tuscan-style, 108–109
Adirondack furniture, 79
Aging techniques, 52, 112, 136, 165, 181, 184–185
Alabaster, 58
Antiques
  beds, 45
  benches, 38
  buffets, 180
  chairs, 169, 181
  contemporary arrangements of, 95
  linens and lace, 147
  quilts, 45
  wicker furniture, 80–81
Architectural fragments, 23, 117, 124, 152, 153
Art, 34, 35, 38, 39, 43, 73, 77, 94, 103, 156, 160, 170
Arts and Crafts-style, 110
Asian touches, 62, 197, 198–199

B

Baker's racks, 92
Bamboo shades, 112, 170–171
Baths
  claw-foot tubs in, 44, 116, 131
  French Louisiana-style, 44
  old-world-style, 112, 116

Beaded board, 156
Bedrooms
  Asian-style, 62
  country cottage-style, 200–201
  Country French-style, 146, 147
  Edwardian, 196–197
  exotic, 198–199, 204–205
  French-style, 63, 128, 194–195, 202–203
  furniture for, 28, 29, 46–47, 113–115, 128–129, 200, 206
  girls', 130–131
  lush, 206–207
  1930s glamorous, 208–209
  old-world-style, 114–115
  romantic touches in, 11–12, 192–211
  Scottish Highlands-style, 76–77
  Swedish-style, 210–211
Beds
  antique, 45
  canopied, 130, 146
  daybeds, 130, 139, 152, 209
  decoupaged, 199
  four-poster, 200–201, 206–207
  Gothic-style, 76
  iron, 45, 115, 146, 147
  paneled, 113
  plantation, 47
  sleigh, 210–211
  vintage, 28
Benches, 38, 125, 202
Botanical art, 160–161, 186
Breakfronts, Gothic-style, 72
Buffets, 43, 175, 180

C

California cottage style, 170–171
California Tuscan-style, 100–117
Candelabras and candleholders, 19, 31, 104, 155, 208
Candlesticks, 31
Chairs
  bamboo, 138–139
  Italian, 29, 42
  Louis XVI-style, 23, 27, 95, 175, 194, 195
  lyre-back, 169
  Queen Anne-style, 94, 189
  twig, 70
  wicker, 80–81, 166, 176
  wing, 60–61, 189
  woven Mexican, 57
Chaise lounges, 191
Chandeliers, 60, 185
  cottage-style, 182

crystal, 128, 133, 175, 177, 189
  gilded, 21, 105
  iron, 42, 43, 79, 92, 109, 175, 190
  pearl-trimmed, 137
  starburst candle, 209
Charleston stable conversion, 84–99
Collectibles
  bronze figures, 87, 88, 90
  candles and candlesticks, 31
  mercury glass, 153
  textiles, 136, 142, 144, 145, 149
  white porcelains, 140, 143
Colors, 12
  accent, 86, 87, 98–99, 194–195, 198, 199
  black, 86, 95, 98–99, 195, 198
  for comfort, 202
  Edwardian, 196, 197
  garden-style, 178
  gold, 91, 194–195, 198
  jewel, 196, 197
  monochromatic schemes, 136
  neutral, 87, 129
  pink, 75, 78
  red, 35, 60–61
  restrained, 186
  starting points for, 174
  Western-style, 180–181
  white, 18, 20–23, 27, 152, 194
Cottages
  in Dallas, 134–149
  in Maine, 66–83
  in Minneapolis, 118–133
  seaside, 156–157
  Tudor, 118–133
  in Washington, 50–65
Cottage style, 166, 170–171, 182–183, 200–201
Crystal, 58, 59, 133, 143

D–E

Dallas cottage, 134–149
Daybeds, 130, 139, 152, 209
Desks, 111, 206
Dining rooms
  colors in, 93, 186–187
  cottage-style, 182–183
  dramatic, 188–189, 190
  eclectic, 121, 174–175
  floral themes in, 177, 182–183, 187
  furniture for, 42–43, 68–71, 92–93, 121, 137–139
  garden-style, 176–179
  minimalism in, 190–191
  old-world-style, 121

red, 35, 36, 60–61
  romantic touches in, 12, 60–61, 174–191
  Tuscan-style, 102, 103–105
  Western-style, 180–181
  white, 22–23, 27
Draperies
  English country-style, 174, 175
  pinch-pleat, 202–203, 205
  sheer, 39, 45, 162–163, 169, 204–205, 208, 210–211
  silk, 153
  softening furniture with, 204
  velvet portiere, 105
Dry sinks, 177
Eclecticism, 52, 54–55
Edwardian style, 196–197
English romantic style, 8, 174–175, 196–197
European continental style, 174–175

F–G

Fabrics, 40
  as accents, 102
  antique, 36–37
  floral, 160–161
  lush, 206–207
  mixing, 113, 122–123, 124, 170, 171
  softening rooms with, 204, 206, 208
Fleur-de-lis, 143
Fleurettes, 143
Floors
  diamond motif on, 157
  hand-painted, 52, 158–159
  wood, 210
Floral themes, 68, 82–83, 126–127, 143
  in bedrooms, 79, 200, 204–205
  in dining rooms, 69–71, 177, 182–183
  in kitchens, 79
  in living rooms, 122–124, 160–161
Flowers, 26, 59, 83, 126–127, 143
French doors, 111
French romantic style, 8, 44, 143, 168–169, 202–203
Furniture. *See also specific pieces*
  antique, 38, 53, 80–81, 95, 169, 180, 181
  arranging, 161
  campaign, 196, 197
  gilded, 89
  large-scale, 106–107

mixing styles of, 52, 54–55, 182–183
neoclassical-style, 184
painted, 114, 157, 170, 171, 200
wicker, 80–81, 166, 176
Garden elements, 127, 178–179
Garden style, 166, 176–179
Gothic furniture, 72, 76

Handwriting, 59, 65
Headboards, painted, 128
Hollywood style, 162–163
Home offices, 158–159
Italian classicism, 117
Italian romantic style, 11
Kitchens, 79, 110, 125
Libraries, 164
Lighting, 39, 102, 178, 207
Linens and lace, 136, 141, 142, 146, 147, 149, 200–201
Living rooms
  artifacts in, 56
  California cottage-style, 170–171
  cottage-style, 122–123, 124
  floral themes in, 160–161
  furniture for, 36–37
  Moderne-inspired, 162–163
  nautical themes in, 157
  red, 36, 37
  romantic touches in, 12, 152 171
  summerhouse-style, 72–73
  Tuscan-style, 106–107, 165
  updated traditional style, 88–89
  white schemes in, 20–21 152–153
Loggias, 57, 102
Louisiana plantation, 32–49
Louis XVI-style chairs, 23, 27, 95, 175, 194, 195

M-O

Maine cottage, 66–83
Majolica, 70, 71
Marbleizing, 168, 169
Mercury glass, 153
Mica lampshades, 110
Minimalism, 86, 190–191
Minneapolis Tudor cottage, 118–133
Mirrors, 20, 22, 53, 95, 121, 191, 194, 201, 208–209
Moderne style, 162–163
Monochromatic schemes, 136
Murals, 164

Nature, orientation to, 34, 49, 190, 210
Nautical themes, 156, 157
Needlecraft, 69
Old-West style, 154
Old-world style, 100–117, 118–133
Outdoors
  furniture for, 112
  orientation to, 34, 49, 125
  romantic touches in, 12

P-R

Patterns, mixing, 161
Pillows, 36–37, 96, 161
Porcelain, 140, 143, 161
Porches, 79, 80–81
Portuguese romantic style, 11
Pottery, 44
Queen Anne-style chairs, 94, 189
Quilts, 45, 79
Romantic style, history and characteristics of, 8–13
Rosecliffe Cottage, 66–83
Rugs
  French Aubusson, 22, 122 123, 124
  Jaipur, 105
  needlepoint, 28
  sisal, 162–163, 196
  tribal, 181

San Diego villa, 100–117
Scandinavian romantic style, 11, 210–211
Sconces, 103, 105, 137, 194
Scottish Highlands-style, 74, 76–77
Screens, Victorian, 70
Sculptures, 24–25
Seashore cottage-style, 156
Settees, 96
Shades, bamboo, 112, 170–171
Shutters, plantation, 96
Sideboards, 19, 20, 69
Silver, 58, 104
Sitting rooms, 38, 39, 53, 54–55, 78, 140–141
Slipcovers, 35, 39, 60–61, 97, 122–123, 200
Sonoma cottage, 16–31
Southwest style, 180–181
Spanish romantic style, 11
Staffordshire figurines, 74, 78, 82, 161
Swedish style, 210–211

T-V

Tables
  Florentine, 171
  French wine-tasting, 42, 43
  Italian, 92–93
  metal-clad, 137–139
  pedestal, 120–121, 164, 181
Table settings, 138, 142
Tapestries, 19
Terraces, 112
Textiles, as collections, 136, 142, 144, 145, 149
Textures, mixing, 126, 136
Topiaries, 43, 44
Transferware, 78
Tubs, claw-foot, 44, 116, 131
Tudor cottage, 118–133
Tulle, 61
Tuscan style, 100–117, 164–165
Vanities, 29, 97, 201
Victorian style, 154–155

W-Z

Wallpaper, 179, 182, 183, 196, 197
Wall treatments
  aging, 144–145, 180, 181, 184–185
  hand-painted, 210–211
  stripes, 199
Washington cottage, 50–65
Western style, 180–181
Wicker furniture, 80–81, 166, 176
Window treatments
  bamboo shades, 112, 170–171
  cafe curtains, 141
  cottage-style, 182
  dramatic, 188–189
  English country-style, 174, 175
  garden-style, 176, 177, 178
  linen and lace panels, 141
  pinch-pleat draperies, 202–203, 205
  plantation shutters, 96
  sheer draperies, 39, 45, 162–163, 169, 204–205, 208, 210–211
  silk draperies, 153
  softening furniture with, 204
  swags, 194–195, 205
  tasseled and trimmed, 129
  valances, 174, 175
Words, 59, 65

Credits

Pages 16-31 Sonoma Cottage Reborn
Design: Lorraine Egidio, Il Nido Nel Giardino, 354 E. Napa St., Sonoma, CA 95476. Regional editor: Carla Howard; Photography: Bill Holt.

Pages 32-49 Louisiana Lake Views
Design: Rebecca Vizard, Rt. 1, Locustland Plantation, St. Joseph, LA 71366, 318/766-4950; fax: 318/766-4954; www.bviz.com. Art: Ann Connelly Fine Art, 2347 Christian St., Baton Rouge, LA 70808, 225/336-0204. Regional contributor: Colleen Scully; Photography: Gordon Beall.

Pages 50-65 Artwork and Artifacts
Design and art: Maureen O'Brien. Regional contributors: Colleen Sculley and Linda Krinn; Photography: Gordon Beall.

Pages 66-83 Fairies and Flowers
Design: Cornelia Covington Smithwick, ASID, Covington Design Associates Inc., 3562 St. Johns Ave., Jacksonville, FL 32205; 904/388-0208. Regional contributor: Susan Stiles Dowell; Photography: Gordon Beall.

Pages 84-99 When Romance Returns
Design: Meredith Dunnan, 2 Water St., Charleston, SC 29401; 843-853-1271. Zinn Rug Gallery (living room rug), 76 Wentworth St., Charleston, SC 29401; 843/577-0300. Yves Delorme (linens), 246 King St., Charleston, SC 29401; 843/853-4331. Regional editor: Lynn McBride; Photography: Gordon Beall.

Pages 100-117 Tuscany Inspired Villa
Architecture: Drexel Patterson, AIA, Tony Crisafi, AIA, Island Architects, 7632 Herschel Ave., LaJolla, CA 92037; 800/316-1776. Design: Constance Noah, Constance Noah Interior Design, 2019 Soledad Ave., LaJolla, CA 92037; 858/459-7051. Regional editor: Andrea Caughey; Photography: Bill Holt.

Pages 118-133 Freshly Edited Opulence
Design: Casabella, 5027 France Ave S., Edina, MN 55410, 612/927-4875. Regional editor: Tangi Schaapveld; Photography: Bill Holt.

Pages 134-149 Linens and Lace
Design: Charlotte Comer, ASID, Charlotte Comer Interiors Inc., 703 McKinney Ave., Suite 314, LB 125, Dallas, TX 75202, 214/953-0855. Regional editor: Diane Carroll; Photography: Gordon Beall.

Pages 152-153: Design: Martha James, 236 Upton Ave., Minneapolis, MN 55405, 612/374-9237. Regional editor: Tangi Schaapveld; Photography: Bill Holt.

Pages 198-199: Design: Camille Saum Interior Design, 7503 Fairfax Rd., Bethesda, MD 20814; 301/657-9817; fax: 301/718-8155. Regional contributor: Linda Krinn; Photography: Ross Chappell.

Pages 202-203: Design: David A. Herchik, JDS Designs Inc., 528 8th St., N.E., Washington, DC 20002; 202/543-8631.

ROMANTIC
Style